BATTLE FOR HEARTS & MINDS

from North East to Kashmir and beyond

Major General Dipak Mukherjee

Vitastaa

Let Knowledge Spread

Published by
Renu Kaul Verma
Vitastaa Publishing Pvt Ltd
2/15, Ansari Road, Daryaganj
New Delhi - 110 002
info@vitastapublishing.com

ISBN 978-93-82711-90-2

First Edition 2016

2nd Reprint 2019

MRP ₹425

Typeset by Vit Press
Printed by Vikas Computer and Printers

Contents

To the young generations of India who have to carry the cross of inadequate delivery of governance for the last seven decades

Acknowledgements

I thank my battalion, the 9th Battalion Bihar Regiment, and Mohan Sunhare, my technical assistant in Mhow for handling the entire computer operations in preparation of this manuscript.

I am extremely grateful to my colleagues and friends, Lt Gen Milan Naidu, PVSM, AVSM, YSM (Retd), Former Vice Chief of Army Staff and Member Armed Forces Tribunal, Lt Gen NS Ghei, AVSM, Commandant, National Defence College, New Delhi and Lt Gen GS Chandel, YSM (DGRR & COBR) Director General Rashtriya Rifles. for their valued inputs on my book. I profusely thank Indrani Bagchi, Diplomatic Editor, *The Times of India*, for having encouraged me to write this book. Her comments on the book means a lot to me.

I can never thank enough my wife Chhanda, daughter Pia and her husband Akilesh Eswaran in London, and my son Pratim and his wife Gaurangi in Malaysia. Their constant support and encouragement while trying to write this book were invaluable.

I am grateful to my publisher Renu Kaul Verma for the professionalism displayed while scrutinising the synopsis and the manuscript. She encouraged me to build upon the theme. I thank my editor Papri Sri Raman for her constant inputs, her enthusiasm made me work harder. Her suggestions to add value to the script were very useful. She is untiring, diligent and an evolved editor. I also thank Vitastaa's production staff for their effort.

...that strict, menacing, inaccessible, and elusive line that separates two enemy armies became all the more clearly felt. One step beyond that line, reminiscent of the line separating the living from the dead, and it's the unknown, suffering and death. And what is there? Who is there? There, beyond this field, and the tree, and the roof lit by the sun? No one knows, and you would like to know; and you're afraid to cross that line, and would like to cross it; and you know that sooner or later you will have to cross it and find out what is there on the other side of the line, as you will inevitably find out what is there on the other side of death.

—Lev Tolstoy

Foreword

Sword of the thinking soldier

I consider it a great honour to be asked to write a Foreword for the book, *Battle for Hearts & Minds from North East to Kashmir and beyond.* The author, General Dipak Mukherjee, is a dear friend and a colleague. Right from his early days Dipak, or as he was known to us–Dadu, was an intellectual soldier. He always questioned the larger aspect of ethics, morality and appropriateness of any action. It was always a profound experience to interact with him.

To my mind, Dadu is eminently qualified to write on the aspects of governance—deficit of which invariably leads to violence and discontent. Thereafter, it devolves on the Security Forces to undertake the 'battle for hearts and minds'.

A lucid Boswell, he covers the entire spectrum of conflict situations in India, with important lessons for all officials, military and civil. Fate ensured that Mukherjee was posted wherever conflict situations arose or were prevalent. One gets an excellent 'worm's view' of the issues other than operational, which had an important bearing on the success of his missions. His experiences in Nagaland, under the guidance of the benign Commanding Officer Lt Col Beglin, are most educative.

The 1971 Operations in Bangladesh is a classic example of the role of 'civic affairs' in operations when the Indian Armed Forces are operating beyond our territories. In the Indian context, we need to remember this lesson for all 'out of area operations'. Success of 'civic action' is as important, if not less, than the actual operational successes.

The chapter on Sri Lanka Peace Keeping Operations makes very interesting reading. As the Commanding Officer, one is the 'Mai-Baap' of all ranks in the unit. The 'buck stops here'. His marvelous innings as the Commanding Officer in operations in Sri Lanka is certainly an additional feather in his cap. Purely from operational point of view, it is discernible to even a lay man, that we violated the 'basic principles of war' and disregarded the lessons learnt earlier in 1971. His research into the genesis of conflict reveals a very different aspect, which had not been studied and was not considered in India's calculations. This, perhaps, holds good even now.

His exposure to the National Defence College was indeed enlightening. Now, he was better equipped to handle the Kashmir operations in the Tangdhar Valley of Kashmir and subsequently the Counter-Terrorism Force in the valley. Mukherjee's insight into the problem is amazing. His actions should serve as a bench-mark for all those who still operate in those areas.

It is for the nation's consideration that India exposes its military leadership early in their career to other aspects of governance, finance, management and administration, to make them better-equipped to perform their basic role. The War Colleges of the Indian Army, Navy and the Air Force are ideal platforms to expose mid-level officers to such an environment.

To my mind, Dadu's 'swan song' has been his tenure with Shree Maheshwar Hydel Power Corporation Ltd as the Advisor for Community Developmental Projects. Here, he came face-to-face with the actual situation as existing in the 'civvy street'. His observations and recommendations are truly profound. I would recommend that not only just the military, but the civil administrators too, make a note of the conditions that exists, which impinge on the nation's march towards progress and prosperity.

Honestly, I could not put down the script. I re-read it with deliberation before writing the foreword. The book truly deserves to be classified as a reference-book and is a 'must read' for all aspiring leaders.

—Lt Gen Milan Lalitkumar Naidu
PVSM, AVSM, YSM (Retd),
Former Vice Chief of Army Staff
and Member, Armed Forces Tribunal

Penning the essence of military life

This book, so aptly titled, takes us through a vast canvas, ranging from the Naga Hills, Manipur, Bangladesh, Sri Lanka to Jammu and Kashmir. Written in a simple style, the book is anchored in the realities of life as seen from the author's eyes and gives an excellent understanding of nature, culture, people, conflict and how they all influence each other. It gives us the essence of military life in a most endearing manner. Interspersed with interesting anecdotes starting from childish school-time pranks, it makes this noblest of professions appear as a beautiful way of life, full of joy de vivre, strength of character and substance.

The narrative is strung together with the central theme of winning 'Hearts and Minds' in any situation. This is a concept that has been the bedrock of India's military, with a strong conviction in it, which sets it apart from other militaries of the region. It brings out the strength of the Indian Army's soft power and the invaluable contribution and sacrifices it has made in the process of nation-building since 1947, by filling the gaps in governance in the remote areas of our nation, with their logistical nightmares.

The book, in its riveting narrative, highlights the essence of national security, democracy and how a soldier-scholar perceives them. Based on life-time observations and learnings of a hard-core professional, who has been part of some of the most momentous military events of our region, this book is interesting reading and a must for all aspiring, young and seasoned soldiers and all others who love their nation.

—Lt Gen NS Ghei, AVSM
Commandant, National Defence College, New Delhi

Nation First, with feet firmly on the ground

Soldiers tend to be delectably frank. They straddle a profession which has little scope for shades of grey; the mission must be clear and simple. If one comes across rather simplistic narratives on governance and nation building, national security and notions of welfare from old soldiers, one must countenance their professional ethos.

So it is with this outstanding work by Major General Dipak Mukherjee, titled *Battle for Hearts & Minds from North East to Kashmir and beyond.*

General Mukherjee has chosen to bare his heart after retirement, putting across real-life experiences at grassroots level in counter-insurgency and border conflicts, covering a very large canvas. From North East to Kashmir, the book puts across a perspective only a ground soldier can narrate, with both feet firmly on the ground. Sample this, 'This narrative brings out the fact that winning the hearts and minds of Nagas, Mizos and later Manipuris were not very difficult tasks. India did not do it….' Quick in arriving at judgments, put across by an impassioned soldier who sees fleeting opportunities slip by as policymakers in far off capitals argue and dither, this is a book that makes one think. The soldier is frustrated that steps and measures that appear so mundane and crystal clear are messed up. In the process, insurgencies get larger, withering the nascent state even before it finds its feet on the ground.

The book is full of lively anecdotes that would regale its readers, giving a rare view of life in cantonments and messes, inside operations rooms and trenches, facing enemy bullets and own citizens' ire. The reader is left with an overwhelming notion of compassion and sense of belonging that the Indian Army has displayed through the seven decades of independent India, whether deployed at home or abroad.

The author brings on the table a ring-side view of the Sri Lanka intervention where he led his battalion as a Commanding Officer. On hindsight, he is unforgiving about the decision-making process that led to this operation, 'India and strategic insight appeared to be parallel lines, never seeming to meet.'

The Kashmir cauldron gets similar incisive deliberation and analysis, forcefully arguing his case for a more robust and stable policy continuum. Beyond the army, the General moves into the civvy street as an adviser on rehabilitation in deep interiors of peninsular India. Here too, the machinations of the stakeholders, the corporate, the politicians, the goons and the silent suffering of the toiling masses reminds one of Arundhati Roy in her tome, *Listening to the Grasshoppers.* Of course, this is no left-leaning perspective of an accomplished author like Roy, but a very charming yet simplistic discourse as only a soldier can feel.

General Mukherjee does yeomen service to the coming generations of policymakers and lay readers alike by putting together a powerful and spellbinding narrative. The book is sure to fire the readers' imagination and this by itself would more than achieve the very aim of the author, **Nation First.**

—Lt Gen GS Chandel
YSM, DGRR & COBR
Director General Rashtriya Rifles and
Colonel of the Bihar Regiment

Who is our Raavan?

Winning hearts and minds is the holy grail for nations waging wars through the ages. It's not overwhelming military might alone that wins wars—they can win the conflict, but rarely the war.

General Dipak Mukherjee, whose distinguished military career gave him a participant's role in almost all of India's major battles after independence, shares his valuable and almost unique insight into how the Indian Army actually won wars on the ground. When the moral compass was steady, as in Nagaland, in the 1950s and '60s or during the Bangladesh war of 1971, the Indian Army achieved victories far bigger than military surrenders.

In Nagaland, it took anti-malaria tablets and medical camps among the Naga tribes to bring them around to accepting the presence of the Indian Army. As Gen Mukherjee recounts, during one of the first conversations with Naga tribe-leaders, it became evident that for these proud people, their first brush with the Indian state was not one that provided basic necessities, but the menacing rifle-toting soldier. 'Calling up the Armed Forces was the easiest way to respond wherein the responsibilities were outsourced, without any other nation-building efforts like providing development and good governance. None of these babus had visited any area beyond Guwahati.'

In Bangladesh, the Army came upon a village which had lynched four fleeing Pakistani soldiers to death. The Indians rescued the last two from a very painful end, at a time when triumphalism could have overtaken everything. The Baloch jawans, who Mukherjee's men saved, became prisoners of war, but they went home, unlike the Indian POWs in Pakistan, a fact that leaves a bitter taste with him.

But in Sri Lanka, India's moral compass was severely tested. As one havildar said, 'Sahib, we all are now in Sri Lanka. Last time in ancient history, Ram came here with his army to fight Raavan. Can you tell us, who is our Raavan here?'

The battle for hearts and minds will continue to inform our understanding of wars. In this journey, General Mukherjee's insights are a valuable milestone.

—Indrani Bagchi,
Diplomatic Editor, *The Times of India*

Preface

As a twelve-year-old child, I was a compulsive dreamer, a romantic who was perpetually attracted by big lovely female eyes. The period was 1950s, in a young, newly-created country. I was ideally representative of the times when India was awakened, dreaming or even fantasising about a great future. The Bombay film industry with big-eyed, wide-hipped, buxom heroines and funny-looking heroes were busy selling dreams. Perhaps the first reaction of liberated citizens of any ancient civilisation, repeatedly conquered and colonised, would be quite similar. Poets, writers, entertainers, artistes, scientists, youths were all at their creative mode, dreaming, romanticising the future that lay ahead.

The 1950s were rather easy-spaced and, therefore, deceptive. Illusion predominated realism. Major events in the international environment, particularly in the USA, Soviet Union and the Eastern Block, China, Middle East were not adequately factored in into India's thinking. Only a few leaders of eminence in India were capable of doing so. They were too overwhelmed with nation-building processes at that time. During those early years after independence, having a big-sized, wooden-framed HMV radio at home was a symbol of prestige as was children going to a convent school in a formal school bus. Job environment was largely of government service, public sector enterprises, doctors and engineers. 'Job' largely meant a

10 am to 5 pm stint, both sharp. It was so easy-paced wherein, on the way home, government employees would be spotted shopping for vegetables and other items of domestic use, in a very leisurely manner.

Getting a government job guaranteed ultimate job security, a steady, routine, easy-going lifestyle. It implied prestige, perks, life-long pension, family pension for the widow. Normally, getting a government job promptly led to marriage within a few months. Except in some regions in the North, North West and western parts of India, joining the Army was generally not popular. Those days, understanding of 'national security' was largely dominated by threats from Pakistan and protection of Kashmir. India was yet to learn the lexicon of larger issues of national security like geostrategy, geoeconomics, national interests, global power play etc, till the Chinese taught India her first lesson in 1962.

As a child, I was deeply moved by patriotic Hindi movie songs of the 1950s. One such song was:

> *Jaago tumko Baapu ki jagir ki raksha karni hai.*
> *Jaago laakhon logon ki taqdeer ki raksha karni hai.*
> *Abhi abhi jo bani hai us tasveer ki raksha karni hai.*
> *Hoshiar, tumko apni Kashmir ki raksha karni hai.*
> *Saari duniya jal uthti hai mutthi bhar angaaron se,*
> *Sambhal ke rahna apne ghar main chhupe hue*
> *hathyaron se.*
>
> Awaken O India, you have to protect the land of Gandhi, awaken to transform the destiny of lakhs of people, the newly emerged map of India has to be protected. Hark! Beware! You have to protect our Kashmir. The whole world may burn from a spark of fire. Be careful of the hidden traitors within our country.

Another song depicting the feelings of a rickshaw-puller also seemed very revealing:

> I am a rickshaw-puller, a rickshaw-puller
> My two feet make for four wheels of the rickshaw...
> Why is there so much shortage of everything in this world?
> Who has stolen all these things, where is it all hidden?

Yet another song from a Bollywood film deeply influenced my generation. The film showed a poor, unemployed actor, the hero, roaming around the streets of Bombay singing this song. The black and white camera showed flashes of abject poverty on the streets, bylanes, slums while some extremely rich people were arrogantly enjoying their wealth, not even noticing the extreme poverty all around.

Jinhe naaz hai Hind par woh kaahan hai,
Kaahan hai, kaahan hai, kaahan hai?

Where are those people who are proud of India,
Where are they, where are they, where are they?

How relevant are these songs even today? Perhaps they are even more relevant than they were ever before.

The very important aspect of integrating the Hearts and Minds of a multicultural, multilingual, multiethnic and multireligious demography got ignored amidst the cacophony of the first two decades after India's independence from British rule. Each decade became a reality check. This laid the foundation for future serious internal security problems. The hearts and minds of an aspirational people were aching amidst poor delivery of governance and associated corruption. Government servants became masters at their bureaucratic worst, with British bosses and their checks and balances gone. They aped all the superficial aspects of their British masters but ignored the British work ethos, character qualities and patriotism towards their motherland.

The hearts and minds of the people of the North East were never in sync with the rest of peninsular India, even in British India. China actively supported insurgencies in this region to keep a good portion of Indian troops occupied in internal security tasks. Thankfully, Kashmir on the western front was peaceful.

This narrative brings out the fact that winning the hearts and minds of Nagas, Mizos and later Manipuris were not very difficult tasks. India did not do it. The national intent and focus were different. The distance between Delhi, Guwahati, Imphal and Kohima was geographically very far and mentally even more remote. Politics was shortsighted, if not often totally blinkered.

The period from 1950s to 1980s was opportunity for India to amalgamate the people of Kashmir into the national mainstream. This was not to be. In India, politics dominates national interests and this big door of opportunity was not utilised. My story describes this situation through live experiences, perceptions based on ground situations, which are quite revealing.

The decade of the 1970s was very significant. The story covers events and perceptions of the young men who lived through it at the grassroots level. While India was slowly moving through its nation-building process in an error-prone manner, Pakistan was committing greater blunders. The hearts and minds of East Pakistanis were ignited by grave atrocities of unimaginable proportions perpetrated on the Bengali people by the Pakistan Army. Due to a democratic political setup, the then-Indian government had some fear about the anger of the Indian masses due to the atrocities the neighbouring people had to suffer. When Pakistan, masquerading as a democracy while dominated by its Army, decided to brutally suppress its Bengali citizens (over ninety per cent of whom were Muslims), Indian and East Pakistani people were embroiled in a war they fought and won together. The story provides some real-time insights and experiences about the hearts and minds of a people, now called Bangladeshis.

The decade of the 1980s were full of strategic errors and miscalculations, when India pretended to become a great power. Its intentions were unrealistic and its comprehensive national power and strategic thinking were far inferior, both qualitatively and quantitatively, to what was needed to realise such a dream.

Sri Lankan Tamils were in open military conflict with their Sinhala administration and nothing short of independence (Eelam) was their demand. Very like the East Pakistani Bengalis were, with their Pakistani administration. They were two neighbours, both with ethnic problems. However, fifteen years later India forgot the lessons learned in Bangladesh. One we helped secede, in another we argued against division. India was sucked into the Sri Lanka cauldron in a rather confused and arrogant manner. The Indian Army became embroiled in intense military confrontation with the Hindu Tamil insurgents in Sri Lanka. The story describes the experiences of our soldiers at grassroots level during the Indian Peace Keeping Force interface.

The 1990s and the 2000s were decades of India's entry, rather belatedly, as a nuclear weapons-holding power. Pakistan's near immediate and similar response deflated India's success in having a n-bomb. Notwithstanding this reality check, India celebrated the occasion at a highly unrealistic pitch. The Kargil conflict of 1999 proved that even two nuclear-armed nations can engage in deadly military conflict of a different kind. This story, in a very revealing, candid manner describes this period. The Kashmir cauldron got a new infusion of blood by this daring operation initiated by Pakistan in Kargil. India, with its nuclear power, was totally reactive, fighting infiltrators on its own territory.

However micro they may appear, the anger and frustration in the hearts and minds of people are dangerous trigger points. In a democracy, they must be attended to in an orderly and timely manner in order to preserve democracy. The story goes on to the interior tribal region of Madhya Pradesh. A hydro-electric project is to submerge over a hundred villages. The story vividly covers the resistance and angst of the villagers so affected. Post-retirement, I happened to be an official at the project and a witness to the people's protest. When deficit of governance across the nation is so all-encompassing and corruption so high, how can thousands of families be shifted, rehabilitated, resettled well in a new locality? The story presents the ground realities of such projects. The role of government, corporate owners of the dam, the affected villagers and the anti-dam NGOs are described vividly and frankly here. What still stands out in all these operations is that the anger in the hearts and minds of the people is a very serious issue.

Having lived and worked, serving in all these parts of the country in various capacities, I could not find clear answers to how to plan and win the Hearts and Minds of people, our own people. In the last chapter, the story moves to an isolated cave around Gangotri where a very spiritual person tries to explain such issues. Still there remains too many questions and too few answers. What stands out is that the quest of delivering 'good governance' must continue, that alone can cool down the angst in the hearts and minds of today's Indians who are not ready to accept the present status quo of '*sab chalta hai*' or everything goes, attitude. This process of good governance and development must move much faster in the second decade of the 21st century than hitherto.

Narendra Modi's mantra for revolutions needed for the growth of the country talks about four types of revolution, based on three colours of the national flag and the blue of the Ashok Chakra:

- Green colour suggests another green revolution, focussing on increased agricultural production, agro-technology, value additions and decentralising of warehousing.
- White colour is for another white revolution, focussing on increasing milk productivity and support system for cattle health.
- Saffron colour suggests an energy revolution, towards renewable energy. It also suggests a renewal of energy of grassroots level of Indians—scientists, industrialists, technicians, bureaucrats, politicians etc.
- The blue colour of the Ashok Chakra suggests a blue revolution in terms of fisheries, underwater resources and control of sea lanes.

Is a major change of status quo in politics, governance and speed of development possible within the democratic setup in India?

Can one leader at the top succeed in this venture in such a vast and chaotic country? Do we have an adequate number of leaders of such vast capability available in our political setup under one banner? Will the people of India rise to fully support such a leader? How many Brutuses are there at the apex level of politics to oppose such a leader and let him down? In short, do we have it in us to take India to its highest level of achievements? These are some of the many questions which only the future can answer. Only a well-organised people's movement and stern demand for good governance and development will bring about a largely peaceful revolution. This is the crux of the story of winning the hearts and minds of our people.

NAGA HILLS

Drums in the Distance

From the solemn gloom of the temple, children run out to sit in the dust. God watches them play and forgets the priest.

—Rabindranath Tagore

I was in charge of a platoon which was in a squad post attending a lecture. It was late September 1968. My battalion of five hundred men had been ordered three weeks ago to move to a place in the middle of nowhere called Tamenglong. We were undergoing training for this posting and I thought, a close look at the distant 'horizon' was not going to be very difficult. I was young, enthusiastic and new to the job.

Tamenglong is one of the remoter hill districts of the remote region of Manipur. Even today, if you go to Tamenglong, you will feel as if you are not in India. New Delhi will seem as remote as Burkina Faso–ever heard of this part of Africa?

Adjoining restive Nagaland in the north, Tamenglong is bound by Imphal district in the south, Assam in the west and Senapati district in the east. This is the distant corner of the country that saw the first insurgency take shape. It is populated by Zelaingrong Nagas who are in majority, along with tribes like Kukis, Chirus and Hmars. The Nagas comprise Rongmei, Liangmei, Zemei and Pumei subtribes.

They are of Tibeto-Burman, Indo-Mongoloid origin. They inhabited the upper course of the Yangtse and the Howang Ho rivers in China during prehistoric times. It was, therefore, perfectly natural that they felt alienated from mainstream India following the subcontinent's independence. The entire Naga and Mizo-populated regions of Assam wanted to secede from India. They never felt that they were a part of India in the first place. The Nagas set up an independent administration called the Federal Government of Nagaland (FGN) in the Naga Hills district of Assam in 1956. This separatist activity spilled over into the four Naga-dominated districts of Manipur also. The base of the FGN was in Ukhrul district, bordering Myanmar (Burma) but Senapati and Tamenglong districts also supported insurgency. These three districts are thickly forested and had hardly any roads even two decades ago. Yomadung and Angouching are the last north-south hills along the border and their forested slopes do not offer easy access to conventional troops. Until the 1980s, all along the border, there used to be only one fair-weather dirt road of Second World War vintage from Kamjong to the Chindwin river valley.

At this time, there was no insurgency in Jammu and Kashmir. The Kashmir valley had settled down in acknowledgement of its accession to India, which was sanctified by their leader and guide Sheikh Abdullah. The raiders sent by Pakistan to capture the valley in 1948, by their ruthless conduct, rapes and loot, got no support from Kashmir. The Indian Army had defeated them soundly after a rather late and hurried action.

Therefore, the Naga rebellion in its North East was the first popular mass uprising and determined insurgency that India faced after independence. This was to continue for many decades thereafter. The term 'terrorism' was not common then. Many facets of this complex insurgency are not known in their micro details. Yet, it is so necessary for the people of India to understand this starting point of Indian insurgency. After all, how on earth does one come to a conclusion if one doesn't have any clue about the beginning? If history is not presented as a recorded story of facts, how can one ever learn from history?

I was a young participant in this starting point of internal challenges to India's national security. My impressions and perceptions are bound to be emotional. Internal security challenges in India, both then and now, at the micro-level, are a lot about emotions, aspirations and perceptions. Let me begin my journey with reliving an insurgency and later, its modern avatar of terrorism in India from 1968 to 2010. This is the crux of my story.

My battalion, the 10th Battalion, the Bihar Regiment, was stationed at Ramgarh when orders came for the unit to move lock, stock and barrel to the Naga Hills. We were given one month to conduct the orientation training. This was to familiarise ourselves with counter-insurgency operations, which were distinct from conventional warfare.

After about three weeks of the orientation training, the Brigade Commander visited the unit to monitor the on-going training. It was to be a day-long event. About five hundred soldiers and officers were out daily in the vast training area of the unit. This entire lot was split into platoons of about twenty soldiers, each carrying out training on different subjects. I was in charge of a platoon.

That day's lecture was being conducted by a smart, slim Havildar who had recently attended a tactical course at the Infantry School near Indore. He was graded as outstanding and was deemed fit to be an instructor at the Infantry School. Such a grading is usually earned by very few students. As per the training programme of the day, this platoon squad post was having a class on 'Horizon'. The subject matter was related to increasing one's ability to analyse the terrain towards the enemy side, and also to correctly assess ranges of various objects and targets.

As and when the Brigade Commander chose to come to our squad post, the Havildar was supposed to commence the lecture by asking the question, '*Jawan, soche aur bataen,* Horizon *kya hota hai?* (Soldiers, what do you understand by the term Horizon?)'

After a small pause, the Havildar would ask a previously-rehearsed soldier to answer. The earmarked soldier would state,

'*Sriman,* Horizon *ka matlab hai ki door disha mein jab hum dekhte hai toh zameen aur aasman milta hua nazar aata hai.* (Sir, Horizon means that when we look at the far distance, the ground and sky appear to be meeting each other.)'

'*Durust hai.* (That is correct)', the Havildar was supposed to reply and then proceed with his lecture.

It was as simple as that, I thought. Usually the Brigade Commander would, after a couple of minutes, move on to other squad posts and training activities laid down for his visit all along the vast, open training area.

Exactly as rehearsed, was what happened initially. Suddenly, the Havildar, in his exuberance to impress the Brigadier and to contribute towards the good name of the unit, exceeded his brief. He asked another soldier to further clarify his understanding of horizon. This was not part of the rehearsed script. To compound matters further, he asked a Jawan who was a wrestler and had hardly attended training, as he was practicing for competitions. That day he was to quietly sit in the squad post.

I had butterflies in my stomach. A major f…up was about to happen. The Commanding Officer gave me a worried look.

The wrestler got up slowly. He knew that the *Izzat* and *Iqbal* of the unit were involved. He gave a dirty look at the Havildar and replied pensively, 'Horizon *to wahi hai jaise ki Jawan ne abhi bataya. Issi ko aur vistaar se samjhne ke lie main to sirf yeh batana chahunga ki door se dekho toh zameen aur aasman milta hua nazar ata hai, lekin nazdik jao to ch…ia ban jate hain.* (When you watch in the far distance, the horizon looks as if the earth and the sky are meeting but if you go toward that horizon, it is a f…er.)'

There was a few seconds of silence. I knew that today's battle was royally f…ed. Who could have foreseen such a situation?

The silence was broken by loud laughter from the Brigade Commander. Just as the Commanding Officer was about to speak, the Brigadier walked up to the wrestler, put his hand on the wrestler's shoulder and complimented him.

'*Shabash Jawan, zindigi mein pehli baar kisi ne mujhe horizon ke bare me itni acchi tarah samjhaya. Yeh pura life hi ek horizon hai.*

Aaj tumne apna paltan ka naam roshan kiya. (Well done soldier. In my life, for the first time someone has explained horizon so well to me. Life itself is like a horizon. Today you have done your unit proud.)'

I thought that the entire episode was a divine intervention wherein a f…up of the highest order was converted into a success story. For the rest of the duration of the inspection, the Brigade Commander remained in an excellent mood and often would chuckle and exclaim, 'This whole life is like a horizon. What a philosophy, so simply explained!'

During that evening, after the inspection was formally over, there was a dinner at the Officers' Mess. I was keen to avoid the Brigade Commander. It wasn't possible. The Brigadier walked up to me and said, 'young man, remember that the first casualty in any battle will be the initial plan. It will always go haywire as soon as the first volley of shots are fired, as soon the first artillery shells drop on your unit. Then you have to trust your men whom you so assiduously trained, motivated and led. They will always rise to the occasion and deliver results, far beyond your expectations. Remember this. Well done.'

The military special train was slowly chugging along during a long journey of five days from Ramgarh near Ranchi. The final destination was the remote terminal station of Dimapore in Nagaland. It was October. Dimapore was a highly malarial area at the foot of the remote and dreaded Naga Hills. We were briefed that Naga militants were extremely crafty, natural hunters who loved the hills and dense jungles and hated the plains as well as the people of the plains. They were fair complexioned, with Mongoloid features while we all were wheatish brown, with very different features which at first sight created a natural, instinctive divide. Our languages, our food habits, our religions, our way of thinking, our perceptions, in fact, every aspect of being was vastly different.

When Alexander descended on India, the local people would have seen handsome, fair, superior-looking soldiers and were perhaps overawed. The Nagas had a rather different experience in the early 1960s, when they first saw the Indian Army's induction into Nagaland.

The divide between us and them appeared to be unbreachable. We were the only organ of the government of independent India who came in such large numbers to a region where governance had not even commenced. Beyond Dimapur, the densely forested Naga Hills looked menacingly impregnable. The rifle of the Indian Army, well-oiled and maintained, the sten Carbines with officers and junior commission officers, the two-inch mortars etc must have overawed them, as did the disciplined, business-like professionalism of this 'foreign' army.

It was not that they had not seen the British Indian Army during the mid 1940s. They had seen British officers, some British regiments with many more Indian regiments fighting the Japanese. Nagas disliked the Japanese forces and had provided full support to the British Indian Army. Their support helped in eventual defeat of the Japanese, even though the Japs had reached Kohima, after which they would have reached the foothills at Dimapur and thereafter the plains of Assam. Resolute acts of valour were displayed by Indian troops, led ably by the British officers. As long as the Indian Army is well-led by officers, they are one of the best in the world. In fact, Indian soldiers were exposed to good officer cadre for a very long period in their history due to British officers. Under them, the Indian soldiers went all over the world from Turkey, Germany, France and North Africa to Burma, Malaya, Indonesia and Korea. As the train reached the rather sorry-looking hot, sultry station of Dimapore, buglers blew the note which signalled that the quick reaction teams (QRTs) would deploy themselves in tactical positions around the train and secure the general area. The next bugle call would make troops come out of their compartments—officers and JCOs, followed by Sergeant Majors of rifle companies. Soon the whole battalion would be out on the platform and hectic activities of unloading the compartments and the wagons would commence.

Life is tough for wives of military personnel. After a peace tenure of about two to three years, units are sent to operational areas for a similar period. Children have to keep changing schools every two to three years. The homes change accordingly. The wives have to manage the children and the home on their own. Most operational field postings were in challenging, crisis-ridden areas where a degree of risk is inevitable, both due to accidents and natural calamities like landslides, heavy snow fall and avalanches, as well as hostile actions of insurgents and the enemy from across the borders. Casualties are inevitable. All married personnel thought and hoped that their wives would manage this change with courage and tenacity.

I walked along the platform supervising the activities of my rifle company along with the company commander, Captain Mauji Ram, a cool Jat from Rajasthan. I saw Lt Col Beglin walking around watching all activities and saluted him. When a battalion commander responsible for over eight hundred men is out on vaguely-described operational tasks, in an undesirable, remote part of the country, he is indeed a very lonely man. He can't even display his nervousness and worries to his subordinates.

Paludrine tablets were the prescribed compulsory anti-malarial medicine which was to be taken twice, every week. Violation of this order was an offence under Section 63 of the Army Act. While reminding the soldiers of this, I told them that as per standing orders, sleeves would have to be rolled down without fail every evening when the bugle sounded last light. Ravi, my colleague, and I would never forget about Army Act Section 63.

It was a Saturday evening, the last at the peace station of Ramgarh cantonment. The short peace tenure was about to end. An adventurous and challenging experience lay ahead on the Naga Hills. To celebrate our departure, Ravi and I decided to ride bicycles through the cantonment area late at night, naked except for underwear. After downing a bottle of beer each, we set forth. It was a thrilling experience. We yelled and cheered, ringing the bell frequently. A few soldiers walking by while returning to barracks from sentry duties watched us in amazement, followed by laughter.

Next morning, the incident was known to the commanding officer, Colonel Beglin. He consulted the adjutant and desired that both the second lieutenants (unfortunate Ravi and I) be marched up to him. The adjutant, in his subtle effort to shield the two young officers, said that there could be some complications in suitably charging us. It would be an embarrassment on a formal chargesheet. So, it was decided to charge us both under Section 63 of the Army Act for not observing anti-malaria precautions by exposing our bodies at night, which amounted to an act 'prejudicial to good order and military discipline'. Both of us were marched into the office of the commanding officer, and let off with a non-recordable minor censure.

For the next one week, the unit camped in the general area of Dimapur railway station. The entire range of provisions and equipment were stacked along one of the side platforms, which served a metre gauge railway line during the Second World War, for the Burma front. Meanwhile, a convoy of over one hundred trucks and assorted vehicles were assembled to take the unit deep into the Naga Hills. To reach Tamenglong in 1968, the last leg of vehicular journey could take only light one-ton trucks and jeeps. So, all heavy trucks had be unloaded at the road head. A painstaking reloading of smaller loads in one-ton trucks and the onwards despatch to Tamenglong took another two weeks.

The troops and officers were to march for eight hours to reach Tamenglong. The misery again started when we reached lock, stock and barrel at Tamenglong. Long columns of hired human porters and mules, carrying stores and equipment, marched off like ants through dense jungles and mountain tracks to reach the six posts perched on various hill tops. These posts would, thereafter, be maintained mainly by air. On reaching the post, an area had to be cleared over which Indian Air Force would paradrop fuel and essential provisions, including the much-awaited meat on hoof (live goats) and rum. An improvised helipad had to be made in each post to enable helicopter landings for casualty evacuations.

In the late 1960s, the North East was clearly not integrated into the national mainstream. The entire State of Assam was too vast an area to be governable from Guwahati, its capital. The Nagas, Mizos and elements in Manipur wanted to secede from India and had taken up arms to achieve independence. The people of the vast plains of Assam had nothing in common with the Nagas, Mizos and Manipuris. The whole arrangement was grossly impractical.

As the battalion moved into remote regions around Tamenglong, I and the other officers and men could see the appalling lack of any sign of governance or government officials. Even the Army, on entering such areas, felt that they were no longer in India. How on earth could the neglected local hill tribes feel or accept that they belonged to a country known as India?

Even the few government officials at the district headquarter of Tamenglong could stay and survive only due to being co-located with the Army Battalion Headquarters. There were no roads at all from the district headquarters to any of the outlying villages of the district. Villagers had no medical, educational or any other facilities. In fact, there was no governance in 1968 in this region by India.

How could people here, for the next few generations, ever feel that they were part of India, I wondered.

There was a huge cultural and civilisational difference with the rest of India. India's history since ancient times had not impacted them. The tribes were a proud lot and they had every right to be so. They had the burden of maintaining their own rich tribal identity while gradually trying to develop a sense of belonging to India. They deserved a well-conceived national effort to help them in this endeavour. This was not forthcoming. How could India fail these fascinating tribes so completely?

The initial response of the local tribes to the presence of the Indian Army was hostile. Unfortunately, after nearly twenty years of India's independence, the only representation of the Government of India, seen by remote villagers were the troops of the Army, with weapons and battle equipment. This was all wrong. It was a strange, shameful and thankless experience. How can a country send its military to an area where it had not even started to provide any semblance of governance? Even due to special circumstances, if it had to send in the military, there ought to have been a well-conceived strategy to establish governance and execute some developmental plans. Nothing like that existed or was implemented. No one was bothered. From our location in Tamenglong, India did look menacing, arrogant and grossly insensitive indeed.

The arrival of the Army was seen as an interference or occupation by the non-tribals living in the Naga areas too. It seemed that India had intruded into their lives by strength of military power. Assam or Guwahati was too distant an entity for the local non-tribal people and India was too unknown for them to comprehend.

As the initial army patrols walking over hills and jungles reached remote little villages, their reception was hostile.

In one such patrol, I had an embarrassing experience. The village was Oinamlong, perched on top of a hill. It had about thirty thatched houses made of wood and bamboo. At the door of each house would hang a head of a hunted animal. As one entered through the door, there was a big room. In the centre was a fireplace, which was always lit while the house was occupied by its family members. Over the fireplace, from the roof hung pieces of meat of various animals. These were raw well-smoked meat.

As I knocked on the door there was no response. I gently opened the door. The entire family was sitting around the fire. One lady was chopping a piece of meat. No one spoke. They did not even look at me or the soldiers who entered with me. There was strange stillness all around. I tried to say something to draw attention. I felt totally rejected. They seemed to despise our very presence.

I noticed an old lady lying on the side. She appeared to be really ill. She was shivering and sweating. I realised that she was suffering from malaria. I offered some paludrine tablets and indicated to another boy to give two tablets to the lady. I left the house along with the soldiers who had to enter along with me as a security precaution.

That night we settled down on the verandah of the local church and the small school of the village, which were thatched huts. Sentries were posted all around. Nagas were adept at sudden attacks if such precaution were not taken.

Next morning a small delegation of tribals appeared. They were smiling. They brought six eggs along with them. We had an interpreter with us. He was a Havildar who had done a course on Nagamese language. The head of the delegation was the Gaon Burra (head of the village). He profusely thanked us for bringing the woman back from certain death due to malaria. Those two paludrine tablets had saved her life.

I cautiously warned him that she must take two tablets for the next three days and then again two more after four days. If she did not, then she will get the malarial bout again. Now the entire village collected together. Four more such malaria-infected cases got treated. Some cases of stomach upsets and skin infection were also treated.

Some children were given medicines for deworming. Now we were treated with smiles. We generally carried *shakarparas* as part of our ration during such patrols. We ate them after brewing some tea, whenever we halted for break while walking for over 15 km each day during such operations to dominate the area. We offered some to the children. As a return gift, the people offered us a huge pumpkin. These tribals will never accept any favour without reciprocating.

We had touched the heart and minds of this remote village with a few paludrine tablets and some medicine for the sick. Very soon, the Naga insurgents would come to know about our visit. May be there would be a few insurgents from this village itself.

We took a couple of local boys to our post on return. Through them we sent back 100 paludrine tablets which were to be handled by the Gaon Burra for helping future malaria cases in the village. Additional medicines for fever, cough and cold, electral salts, digestives were sent. The local boys wrote down the details of how each medicine worked in Nagamese. For a couple of days they stayed in the unit as guests and a medical camp was conducted for them. With this episode, we made our initial impact on the locals. We were determined to carry on with our own battles for winning over the locals slowly and steadily. We had to touch their hearts with kind gestures.

Our commanding officer, Col Beglin, promptly ordered the Quarter Master, Captain Julius Toppno, to stock all the medicines he could collect for treating the civil population. Brigadier Sinha, the scholar-soldier of eminent character, gave orders to the brigade to indent for more medicines under 'Operation Hearts and Minds' as essential part of counter-insurgency military operations.

Our Regimental Medical Officer, Captain Narayanan, rose to the occasion and rendered great service to the locals.

A few months later, based on intelligence reports about presence of Naga insurgents in a specific area, a special patrol under Captain Ravi was moving out of Tamenglong. It was evening time and the patrol had to march for eight hours through the night to reach the area.

As the patrol was going past Tamenglong, a group of two boys and two girls approached Captain Ravi. They told him that the patrol should not leave that night. The two boys were part of the Tamenglong football team, coached and equipped by our unit. The two girls had got their mothers treated for serious stomach ailments. They insisted that an ambush was planned to be laid for this patrol, for which the intelligence input was planted. Capt Ravi spoke on the radio set to Col Beglin, who cancelled the operation. In fact, he ordered another special patrol to be launched from a different post to lay counter-ambush. We did not catch anyone this time, but most probably, the Naga insurgents were confused by our change of plan and melted away into the jungles.

When the people saw that the Army was there to help, they did not wish them to be harmed. They even prevailed upon the insurgents, who were their own people, not to harm the Army. Even the insurgents could not ignore the wishes of the people at times. However, in very rare cases would the local people in the 1960s provide hard intelligence to the Army against their own insurgents. Inter-tribal rivalry was one opportunity for intelligence agencies to get some inputs about insurgent movements.

We realised that had a well-conceived national effort been conducted in the 1960s, in this area, the hearts and minds of the tribal region of Nagaland and Mizoram could have been influenced to a reasonable extent. Military operations, when conducted along with such efforts, would have been more successful. Pure military operations, not backed by good governance, can never be successful in an insurgency environment. Ironically, repeatedly, the Indian Army has had to perform both hard power and soft power roles in dealing with the strange situations they have landed themselves in time and again. Some units, which were not officered well, displayed only hard power. They not only suffered more casualties, but also failed to effectively controlled their areas of responsibility.

Every remote Naga village comprised two distinct parts. One part of the village was the Christian village and the other part, with a gap of a few hundred yards, was the non-Christian part. Both coexisted very peacefully. The Christian part was much cleaner, better organised, with a small church. Children were cleaner and better fed. Pigs, cattle, chicken etc were kept outside the houses. The non-Christian part of the village was extremely dirty, with pigs, dogs etc straying inside the houses. The children looked very dirty, diseased and underfed. Most of the grain was used to brew country liquor. Christians were forbidden to brew more than a specified amount of grain for liquor. The churches were functional on Sundays.

The Army detachments could not help develop admiration and respect for the Christian missionaries who had taken grave risks decades before, to help these tribals. At the same time, we felt ashamed about the utter failure of the Indian government, which had let down these hapless tribals.

The Nagas and other tribes were wonderful people, with a very rich culture and way of life. It was not so difficult to befriend them, provided one was sincere towards them. Any kind and helpful act was always reciprocated by them. In those days, the houses were never locked and there were no cases of theft. The local breed of buffalo was a huge animal called Mithun. Whenever a Mithun was slaughtered for food, the meat was cut into various pieces. The village elder, Gaon Burra, would distribute the chunks of meat for each house. Distribution was always fair.

Luckily, our regiment comprised a fair number of Adivasi Christians from south Bihar. So the battalion had a unit mandir and a church. This helped in establishing good rapport with the Nagas. The fact that the CO of the unit as well as Captain Julius were Christian was a help. Christmas was celebrated in a big way in the unit. A huge celebration took place during Christmas on the only flat area in the vicinity, which was the unit helipad. The Adivasi troops taught the Naga guests their own tribal dances and the Nagas taught them their nice rhythmic dances. So, in a great act of bonhomie, Army jawans danced the Naga dances while local Nagas danced the Adivasi tribal dances. By now, the Battalion had been well accepted by the locals. We had a very capable commanding officer indeed.

Those were the days when people died of malaria there, as no medical facilities existed. The Commanding Officer directed that all long-range patrols (LRPs) would carry hundreds of Paludrin anti-malaria tablets. As patrols reached remote villages, many Nagas suffering from signs of malaria were treated by the trained nursing attendants. Troops carried some other medicines like multi-vitamins, ointments for skin diseases, deworming tablets etc. Serious patients would be brought on improvised stretchers, over long distances, for treatment at the Regimental Aid Post located in the Battalion Headquarters. The unit medical officer, Captain Narayana, a physically-fit officer from the Army Medical Corps, was easily the most popular officer. Once Captain Narayana, while out on a patrol, saw a Naga woman working in a field on a hill slope, develop labour pains. In a nearby thatched hut used to store grains, along with a couple of local women, he helped her deliver a baby boy. This was greatly appreciated.

Seeing the Army do many such kind acts and considering the resulting popularity of the unit, the district administration felt embarrassed and started getting their act together. They informed the bureaucrats sitting in Imphal and Kohima about the situation and demanded that government send them medicines and ensure visits by doctors as well as set up dispensaries in at least a few groups of villages. It took about a year and, at last, a semblance of medical help, grain distribution, veterinary cover as well as the opening of a few schools started to happen in the region.

Under the wise leadership of the Commanding Officer, the unit started small outreach activities like coaching local boys for football, conducting inter-village competitions, training locals in some skills like carpentry, artisan skills and sponsoring a few boys for polytechnic institutions in Imphal, Kohima and Guwahati.

A new District Collector, who was very sincere and honest, was posted. This helped a lot as he brought in some resources and set out to provide government services. Now the other young officers and I realised that good cooperation and closer affiliation between government officials and the Army could be a very effective way of improving the situation in such far-flung remote areas. Just deriding civil servants, without trying to befriend them and understanding their problems, would produce retrograde results.

While all this was happening, regular encounters took place between Army patrols and Naga insurgents. The insurgents were good at jungle warfare; they knew the terrain and were motivated to fight for independence, for their unique way of life. The unit suffered some casualties, while the insurgents would generally escape into the thick jungles. Winning the hearts and minds of the people had to be done by the government through good, honest governance. The Army could only apply a few band aids here and there.

The biggest challenge in the North East appeared to be not the few insurgents, challenging the Union of India. The biggest challenge came from governance deficit, the insincerity of India towards the North East region and bureaucratic arrogance of the largely city-bred government officials.

In fact, non-delivery of good governance appears to be the greatest unpatriotic act in any country. Gradually, clashes with the insurgents became fewer. The main reason was that the local villages were benefitting from our presence and would not provide adequate intelligence to the insurgents. Local support, in totality, is very critical for insurgent operations.

Some Army units which were not very well led by officers, did commit mistakes. There were a few cases of atrocities, excesses and false reporting. In those days, the media in India was very underdeveloped and the region was very remote. Such units tarnished the traditions of the Army. The culpability of such units was no less than the civil administration's. Their acts were grossly unpatriotic; they harmed India's national interests and helped the insurgents and China, which was providing arms, ammunition and training to the insurgents, from the remote jungles of North Burma. The writ of the Burmese government did not run in those areas, during that period. Some such units were caught and faced court martials. Some units also got away.

I felt proud of my Commanding Officer, Col Beglin, and later Col Sawhney. This unit had an excellent bunch of officers, who would never tarnish the name and reputation of the regiment. They would never misuse or misguide their troops. Many of them may not have been brilliant careerists, but God bless them, they were excellent, troop-oriented professionals. Such was the impression formed by young officers like me, Ravi, Katoch, Julius and newly-commissioned Second Lieutenant Mohan Lal.

One fine morning, as I was supervising the construction of a perimeter mud wall around my remote, air-maintained post, which was two day's walk from Tamenglong, I got a call from Ravi, the adjutant of the unit. I was informed that Colonel Beglin would be landing in a chopper after a couple of hours. He would want to address as many local people as possible, for which an interpreter needed to be present. While activating the helipad, I sent for the Gaon Burra. The Gaon Burra is the centre of gravity for all activities of the village. He dressed up very colourfully whenever he had to perform his duties as the head of the village. He, in his traditional dress, would go usually to the highest point of the village and beat a drum. Every note of the drum conveyed a message. He would beat the drum in a particular manner, which would convey that maximum people should converge for a meeting near the church. When a village was rather big, then the same drum beating would be relayed by designated people, so that the entire village got the message. It was a very fascinating method of command, control and coordination. Earlier, these were the means used to warn a village of an impending attack by other tribes. Since each village was located on a hill top, it was possible to place scouts at various tactical locations, warning the village about movement of neighbouring tribesmen as they climbed up towards the village. The forward scouts would relay the warning through typical animal calls and would melt away inside the dense forests, to take on hostile forces from their rear. No wonder that whenever the Indian Army launched painstaking operations against the Naga insurgents, they would not find them anywhere. They would melt away into dense jungles.

Just as I organised a decent number of locals near the church area and returned to the helipad, I could hear the sound of the helicopter approaching. Those days, a commanding officer, more often than not, had to walk for a couple of days to visit a few posts. Rarely would he get a helicopter. This time, my commanding officer managed to get a helicopter ride. Since my post was the farthest to reach, I was honoured with this visit.

As the helicopter landed on the secured helipad, out came the tall, fair, handsome Colonel Beglin, striding towards me. I saluted and shook his extended hand.

'How are you getting along with the locals? I understand it is a difficult job, but it is a challenge worth striving for. To improve the environment, we have to forge good relationships with these people. You would have realised by now that these tribals are a unique lot, with a rich colourful culture. The onus of understanding them, empathising with them and proving to them that we genuinely want to befriend them, lies squarely on our shoulders. We can do our country a great service by winning the hearts and minds of these people', said the Commanding Officer.

'Yes sir. We are trying to do so and slowly we seem to be making some progress. I am sure that we can succeed', I replied.

The interaction with the villagers was very interesting. A community song in Nagamese, welcoming the Colonel, was followed by a systemic tribal dance. The Gaon Burra spoke on behalf of the people and lamented the lack of any government assistance, school and dispensary. He mentioned the fact that the villagers grew lots of oranges, ginger and bamboo products but could not sell them because of the non-existence of any transportation facilities. The young people here had no hopes. If only some hostel facilities were made in Imphal, Kohima and some district headquarters, then the young people could go for higher studies and to learn skills which would help them earn a living. The Gaon Burra thanked the Army for the medical treatment being provided to hundreds of sick people and for the adoption of some villages by our battalion for providing emergency assistances, repair of churches, provision of games kits for children, taking up cases with the government for animal husbandry, fertiliser and opening of a few schools etc. The list of their demands was basic, simple and legitimate. In fact, they were asking for help to survive and get a sense of belonging. They were asking to be governed. Alas, India was unconcerned. The Indian attitude was colonial in spirit.

On returning to the helipad and the waiting helicopter, I saw the worried faces of the crew of the helicopter. They were keen to take off before the unpredictable weather packed up. The Commanding Officer said, 'Son, you can never understand the North East, if you do not appreciate the culture, tradition and ethos of its colourful tribals. They are so unique, so un-Indian and so unlike the plainsmen. They need to be accepted, adopted, owned and nurtured.'

'Yes sir', I replied. 'There are so many tribes and subtribes, each seemingly similar and yet deep down they are so varied that it is difficult to club them in generalities. If one brings representatives of each tribe and forms them into a group, one realises that they cannot relate to each other.'

'Precisely', replied Col Beglin. 'This describes the paradox of North East India. I am no expert on this part of our country, if you can put it that way, based on our little acquired knowledge by being on the ground. In fact, there is no expert on this part of India and that is how it will be for many more decades. The threat to tribal identity and survival can easily transcend national affiliations, not only in this region but also in the interior regions of mainland India.'

'What is going to be worse', continued the Colonel, 'is that over the next couple of years we will learn a lot more about these fascinating people and will bond with them. Then we will leave, taking all this knowledge acquired through hard work, sweat and blood. Our next tenure may well be in Rajasthan or Jammu.'

'But sir', I exclaimed, 'all our elaborate monthly reports and situation reports, carefully collated and summarised will reach the Ministry of Defence through Army Headquarters. Surely they will get our feedback.'

'Who the f..k cares in Delhi about our so-carefully compiled reports on this abandoned part of India', retorted my Commanding Officer with visible sadness. It was 1969.

I was stunned by the sudden burst of candour from the Commanding Officer. I felt that he had bottled up his emotions for quite some time and he let it out in front of a young officer under his command. This was part of the grooming process of his young officer.

The life of an officer on a remote jungle-clad hill top, two days of long walk away from an unmaintained, jeepable road, is a bewildering and amazing experience. Once a month an aeroplane would come, fly around a small clearing near the post twice and on the third approach drop a dozen odd parachutes. Some would nicely land on the helipad, some would drop down all around the nearby areas, while few at times would go down the deep gorges and would never be found. Each parachute contained food, fuel, some valuable rum cases and a few live goats nicely tied up and padded up to avoid being killed due to impact with the rocks. The soldiers would spare no efforts to retrieve the rum and the goats, even if they had to go down gorges and ravines to locate them. If a goat on landing got hurt, it was immediately slaughtered before it died due to injuries, amidst loud cheers from other soldiers. This was because if a goat was already dead on landing, the soldiers would not eat that meat. It would promptly be given to the villagers.

The loneliness of an officer living in an air-maintained post could be pretty jarring at times. This was particularly so after sunset, which happened rather early in the jungles of the North East. There was no electricity. The Sergeant Major used to connect a small bulb with the battery of a radio set, which gave a little light for a couple of hours at the most. Newspapers about ten days old and some old magazines came in once in a while, along with mule columns which brought in essential stores, potatoes, onions, pumpkins and official and personal letters etc. Under such conditions, a tot of rum in the evening, coupled with hot pakoras, was very welcome. The troops believed that with some rum flowing in the blood, it was easier to kill the mosquitos. After biting and sucking the blood, they became drunk, which slowed their escape. If one failed to take the palaudrin tablets as specified, malaria would be sure to visit. To be evacuated on a stretcher with malaria and high fever was a nightmare.

During one such lonely evening, as I sipped a small peg of rum in my bamboo hut, my thoughts went back to my childhood days. How simple and joyful were they! I was in a military boarding school in Dehra Dun, called the Rashtriya Indian Military College (RIMC).

Dormitory life at the RIMC was fun. Till then, I had hardly interacted with real Punjabis. They were an interesting, jovial lot, full of spirit. Cadet Jas Mohinder Singh was a great guy. On the very second day, he handed one end of his pugri to me and said, 'Oye saale, hold this and keep rolling it like this from one end to the other. Don't f..k it up.' I, who for the first time in my life was helping a Sikh to tie his pugri, was still recovering from the shock of the abuse. Jas Mohinder wrapped the other end of the pugri around his forehead, and kept turning his head to wrap up the pugri neatly till he reached me holding the other end. He snatched the last bit of the pugri from me and said, 'B……od, do it better next time.' This experience was a cultural shock. Jas Mohinder and I became great friends soon. He was such a fun-loving guy, with a 'never-say-die' spirit.

'Cutting bounds' was a term used for quietly slipping out of the RIMC complex after dinner, escaping to Dehradun city, to see a 9 pm to 12 am film show and to return back to the dormitory without being caught. It was a thrilling, risky operation as Duty Masters and Seniors Cadet Captains often made surprise visits to the dormitories. Jas Mohinder, Harish and I made an elaborate operational plan to cut bounds to see the film *Chhalia*, starring Raj Kapoor as the hero. Cadets Raman and Bajaj were given the task of ensuring that they handle the duty masters on rounds and ensure that we were not caught. For that, the beds of the 'bound cutters' were camouflaged well with extra pillows tucked in under the blankets and sheets. This was to ensure that under the veil of the mosquito nets, it would look as if someone was sleeping.

Usually the visiting inspectors would randomly flash a torch on a few beds and move on. Around midnight, after which the three bound cutters were expected to return, the security light behind the dormitory would be kept off, indicating that there has been no problem. In case the security light was on, it would indicate trouble.

After dinner, Jas Mohinder, Harish and I, using stealth and field craft, escaped through the canopy of the guava trees, past the football grounds. We reached the rear gate of the boundary wall behind a disused old bungalow which at one time was a teacher's house. One by one, giving each other a few minutes' gap, we climbed over the gate which was always locked.

Now we headed for the small local bazaar. The cycle shop was open. The shopkeeper was a young fellow, who on seeing the three nervous cadets of RIMC, gave a broad grin. He offered the cycles on hire for one fourth of an anna each. One anna was a copper coin with a hole. The cycles sighed that they had seen better times. On the walls of the cycle shop was the photograph of a very similar-looking elderly gentleman with a big grin. He was the father of this young man and he had died a decade ago. He too had been clandestinely giving cycles on hire to previous generations of young Rimcolleans, many now retired generals, for similar purposes. Cutting bounds was a regular tradition.

It took half an hour of cycling by a shortcut to get to Dehradun town. Before entering the premises of the cinema hall, our group stood in a dark corner and watched the crowd waiting outside. The 6 pm to 9 pm show was just over but the entry doors of the hall were closed. Wearing a cap half hiding my face, I joined the crowd and carefully scrutinised the hundred-odd members of the audience. No school teacher or staff member of RIMC was visible. I now felt safe enough to purchase the three tickets in the lower fare stall. I returned to tell the other two that it was okay.

Chhalia was an entertaining movie. However, the fun in cutting bounds lay more in the thrill of the risky venture and of not getting caught. It was an accomplishment which earned professional respect from all occupants of the dormitory.

On our return, depositing the cycles back to the cycle shop owner was the first phase. Our group, with great stealth and field craft, using the intervening terrain to one's advantage, reached a canopy of trees, about 200 metre short of the dormitory. The second phase of the return operation was to observe the security light behind the dormitory. The light was off. Quietly, we three moved with our heads and midriff half bent and entered the dormitory.

Raman was awake. The sentry could not sleep till the three comrades had returned safely from their mission. 'Welcome heroes. Well done. Now change and go to sleep', said Raman sleepily. Jas Mohinder, Harish and I went to the adjacent changing room, took out our pyjamas from the lockers. Our sports shoes, which we wore during the operation, were full of mud and slush, which accrued during our cross country move to and from the cycle shop. It had rained heavily in the interim.

We were so thrilled that we collectively started singing a song from the film, *Chhalia Mera Naam, Chhalna Mera Kaam, Hindu, Muslim, Sikh, Issai, Sabko Mera Salam.*

'Who are these rogues', shouted the House Master, Mr Bisht, who was taking a round in the neighbouring Junior Dorm.

Jas Mohinder, Harish and I froze. We were royally caught. Defeat stared at us from the jaws of victory. Harish murmured, 'We are f... ed. We f...ed it up.' Jas Mohinder cursed, 'Shut up Harish. Think quickly how to avoid the f..k.' Raman had time enough to quickly put on the rear security light and get into the bed.

Mr Bisht looked menacingly at Jas Mohinder. He was surprised to see Harish, who always sported a very innocent look. Then he looked at me sadly, the ace footballer of RIMC, his greatest hope of defeating The Doon School football team during the annual encounter next month.

'How come you three are wearing pyjamas and a wet full shirt at this late hour? Let us go and check the changing room.' The changing room had three wet trousers thrown around hurriedly and mud-coated sports shoes, three wet vests and two underwears. Jas Mohinder was still wearing his wet *kaccha*. It was apparent to me that the game was up.

'You three cut bounds?' bellowed Mr Bisht. 'No Sir', replied Jas Mohinder rather apologetically. 'Sir, we went out for cross-country practice towards the games fields. We are doing this late at night, for the last seven days. We wanted to win the cross-country competition for our House next week.' Jas Mohinder humbly bowed his head.

'Is it true?' asked the House Master staring at me. I glimpsed victory now, from the jaws of defeat. Thanks to my Sardar friend, whose pugri I had been holding for the last two years and getting abused in turn.

'Yes Sir' I replied.

'But why at this unearthly time of the night?' quizzed the House Master.

Harish realised that no one needed to get f...ed now and his brain came alive at its creative best. Putting on his most innocent face, he said, 'Sir, it was my idea to ensure that the other Houses don't come to know about our extra preparation. Surprise is the best weapon in any battle, as we have been taught at RIMC.'

Mr Bisht replied, 'Whether this is true or not, it certainly is a smart thing. I give you the benefit of doubt. It would have been smarter if you all did not sing that song'. He nodded his head pensively and walked away. Needless to say, Mr Bisht had no intention of reporting this matter to the Principal. After all, as the school football coach, he had to preserve his ace footballer and centre forward. RIMC versus Doon School matches were like India-Pakistan contests. Doon School was Pakistan, of course.

Those were the days, I sighed with nostalgia as I downed the last bit of my small peg of rum.

During an operation, with a column of twenty five soldiers, we had cordoned off a remote village at night after a long march of two days. While searching any village in the morning, the procedure was to announce through the Gaon Burra, a call for all women and children to assemble at a central place. While the search would commence in the morning, the women and children would be given a rudimentary medical check and iron tablets were distributed to them. As this was happening, a young insurgent was caught with a pistol. Intelligence reports had indicated the likelihood of three insurgents living in the village. The local police at Tamenglong had provided the photographs. The other two insurgents had escaped the cordon.

Initially the insurgent appeared to be a young man of distressingly few words. I realised that to understand this insurgent, he needed to be provoked and angered. Apparently, he was a man of courage and fortitude. His self-confidence was amazing, bordering on arrogance, even when he had been captured. 'What is your name?' I queried. 'I am L Theubam and I fight for freedom to follow our way of life', was the stubborn reply.

'Why have you become an insurgent?' I asked. The local church priest was interpreting our conversation. 'I am a proud Rongmei Naga and am free to roam around on my land', replied the insurgent.

'Why are you carrying a pistol with you?'

'Why are you all roaming around this region armed with so many weapons? This is our land', was the stoic reply.

'You want to fight the Indian Army?' I provoked.

He smiled and retorted, 'We were living here freely in our own land. You all suddenly come with thousands of soldiers and weapons. You come here to kill us, you disturb our lives. We do not know who you are, why you occupy our region. We do not like you. We never were part of your culture, your way of life. It is you and your country which is fighting us.'

I found the young Theubom embedded in his distinct separate ethnicity, ideology and perceptions. 'Where are the other two hostiles who were with you? What weapons do they carry? In which village do they live? How many of you operate in this area?', I asked in a loud voice, this time.

'Betraying comrades may be normal in your part of the world. We tribals never do that. Just as we can kill our enemies, we can also die fighting them. We are one for all and all for one, Sir. This is our kingdom. If we do not fight for it, who will?', was the ebullient response.

I was getting impressed with the young insurgent. If these people got amalgamated with mainstream India and were granted the security of their ethnic identity, if they were well and justly governed, they could be a great asset to the nation in a few decades, I thought. They could be a rich crop for raising a fighting fit Naga Regiment or as excellent sportsmen. Instead of fighting against the Indian Union, they could well be fighting for it on the North East borders.

Suddenly, the reality of our conversation struck me. I felt that I was talking as one soldier to another. Deep inside me, I did not feel that I was talking to some alien, but to someone who was an Indian, emotionally departed from me. This fellow was a blend of loyalty, fidelity, courage and honour. These tribals possessed unbridled pugnacity. With the infusion of regimentation and discipline, they could be very efficient soldiers. A deep sense of personal honour was embedded in these tribes. This could be productively harnessed.

'Why are you so against India?' I continued.

'How can one be against someone who one does not know anything about? In our minds, we cannot see beyond these hills, jungles, mountains, and neighbouring tribes. If we belonged to something called India, then where has India been? Its existence has not been felt by us for centuries, and particularly for the last twenty years. Suddenly your Army arrives, disturbs our natural existence, and we are told to belong to India. The basic sense of belonging from either side is non-existent. You all, Sir, have occupied our sacred area. You need to withdraw and come back to us after giving us a sense of belonging. You cannot just own us. We have to accept you first. There have to be conditions formalised and negotiations done. We need to know what we would gain by accepting you and what we would lose', replied the insurgent whose eye contact with mine remained steady during this monologue.

'Wow, this fellow has character, equanimity and a solid pair of testicles', I thought. Insurgents in India in the 1960s were not misguided elements roaming around, spreading violence and taking up cudgels with the Government of India. They were the residual product of the incompleteness of India's nation-building process after merely two decades of its independence.

The nation will never fully comprehend and never acknowledge the critical role played by the India military towards its nation-building process and ensuring the integration of the remote region of the North East with mainland India. This was done both by the use of controlled force as well as by trying to win the hearts and minds of the hitherto abandoned populace.

Theubam was treated well. He was disarmingly honest, arguing not with venom and hatred, but from the bottom of his heart. When I explained the whole situation to my commanding officer, Colonel Beglin, he directed me to send Theubam with any returning patrol, to the Battalion Headquarter at Tamenglong.

We had a very farsighted and professionally competent Brigade Commander. Brigadier Sinha had a deep insight about the Nagas and the on-going insurgency. He readily agreed with our suggestion that Theubam should be released with honour. He had given an undertaking that he would live overground and would not directly indulge in violence. He, however, gave it in writing through his village Gaon Burra, that under no circumstances would he reveal any details about his fellow insurgents and betray them. He was in love with a girl named Athuan Lui and intended to raise a family. The cute Athuan Lui and the villagers in surrounding villages appreciated the way the Army handled the situation. Intelligence reports later confirmed the fact that the local insurgent groups acknowledged a grudging respect for the Army. Soon a few insurgents, who were either ill or growing old, surrendered and were allowed to live peacefully in their villages, with similar undertakings. In matters of honour and loyalty, these tribals had a deep value system in the 1960s.

Soon the rapport between our unit and the locals grew and invitations to attend local festivals started coming. During such festivals, we were assured by the locals that being guests, our security was assured and we need not partake in the festivities with our weapons. As per tribal customs, such assurances were inviolable. Even then, we did have security positioned at vantage points, as our rules of engagement did not permit us to violate standard operating procedures.

In one such function, a big group of Naga men, dressed in traditional attire, with spears, arrows, swords and bamboos cut in a manner representing twelve-bore double barrelled guns, presented a fantastic tribal dance. The dance depicted a battle with another tribe.

The dance described a typical battle which was conducted a few decades ago, when head-hunting of a defeated enemy was the norm. The dancers were all in an inebriated state. All had taken a fair amount of a local brew called 'Madhu', which essentially was rice beer. The beer was held in the horns of hunted animals. While the dancing started in slow, rhythmic beats, it gradually increased in speed and was accompanied by wild shrieks in which the audiences laughingly joined in. Coordination of steps and the rhythm was all perfect, despite the fact that the dancers were quite inebriated. It was a fascinating experience with the backdrop of a clear blue sky, a full moon and a glowing fire around which the dance was conducted. Coming from the plains of hinterland India, we felt we were on a different planet.

It was then that I truly appreciated the fact that India does need a few more decades, before it can eventually assimilate these fantastic tribals into its national mainstream. Two decades after independence was too short a period to do so. I felt proud to be part of the initial, virgin attempts of such a long-term process. The only national institution to be able to dare to initiate this process had to be the Indian Army. Will our nation later remember the role we played?

'Don't even dream about this. The country will never acknowledge what we are doing here', said Captain Ravi. 'Meanwhile', added Ravi, 'a miniscule number of ill-led units may give us a bad name by not behaving well with these people and could well bring us to shame.' How right Ravi was! Pre-induction training of at least three months was needed to familiarise the units about the culture, ethos and the value systems of these fascinating people. During such formal institutionalised training, the aspect of winning the hearts and minds of these tribals needed to be emphasised if one wanted to succeed in anti-insurgent operations and to help the nation tackle the complex problem of the North East.

Winning the hearts and minds of the people had to be the centre of gravity for a plethora of comprehensive national efforts to reconcile the remote regions of North East India. There could be no exclusive military solution to insurgency, even though the military had to play a key role. India just has to govern itself well to survive as an entity.

The North East taught India this first basic lesson. Fundamentally, the Nagas and the Mizos taking up arms against Indian occupation in the 1960s was a natural and a legitimate response, when viewed from the perspective of the tribals. It was both a clarion call and a wakeup call for India.

Eventually, every peace enforced purely by military means, sans any genuine delivery of good governance, becomes akin to the peace in a graveyard. The ancient Greeks believed that people who walked into the future, with their eyes closed to the past, lived life dangerously. So, if the past was distorted and was not analysed correctly, it could do grievous damage to the future.

The reality after independence was that vast tracts of the mountainous jungle-clad, remote North East, beyond the plains of Assam, was totally outside the sphere of Indian influence, even more than before the colonisation of India by the British.

Internal instability and insecurity has been India's Achilles heel. These seemingly eternal fault-lines had made India vulnerable to conquests and colonisations, loot and slavery.

Conveniently, after independence, the Indian government has saddled the Indian Army with significant internal security responsibilities, while at the same time it has corrupted and misused its police forces. It was a classical case of outsourcing internal security responsibilities to the military. That is why, at the slightest pretext, the Army gets called in, much before the District Magistrates and Chief Secretaries of States utilise the police forces. This short cut attitude has reduced the urgency to upgrade the police forces and to increase their capabilities or carry out police reforms.

In reality, the neglect of development and natural assimilation of remote regions of India was manifest and the resultant subversion and proxy support of disgruntled elements by outsiders, was extant. There appeared to be no doubt about the fact that Chairman Mao intended to arm Naga and Mizo militants to wage a proxy war in order to bleed India. It was indeed surprising that even a few years after the 1962 war, India was not alert enough towards this development in the North East.

The people of North East tribal areas realised that if India was ready to abandon parts of Arunachal Pradesh during the course of the 1962 war, it would do the same and withdraw if Chinese-sponsored guerrilla war was waged intensively on the Nagaland frontier. Because of this lack of strategic insight and strategic advice, policy-makers in India were not alert to Chinese capabilities and intentions at that point in time. How can one confront an adversary one does not understand?

Therefore, a decade or so after independence, the Indian government's response to the armed insurgency in Nagaland and Mizoram was tragically colonial in nature. The Indian Army was inducted into these regions. The steel frame of India, the Indian Administrative Service, (officers) who were the all-powerful all-rounders, were the singular advisors to the government on strategic matters.

Calling up the Armed Forces was the easiest way to respond wherein the responsibilities were outsourced, without any other nation-building efforts like providing development and good governance. None of these babus had visited any area beyond Guwahati.[1] India had no experts on her tribal regions, with its

---

[1] In 1959, for the first time, the Nehru government asked tribal expert Verrier Elwin, who had done extensive work on the Baigas and Gonds of Central India, to prepare a report on what was then known as North East Frontier Agency. The result was a voluminous study, *A Philosophy for NEFA*. The book was written, presumably, to formulate a policy and a philosophy for the administration of NEFA and to introduce NEFA to non-local government officials. One interesting feature of the book is a historical review of some of the thinking then about the character and merits of 'native' peoples, in which the opinions of foreign scholars like Montaigne, Spenser, Shakespeare, Rousseau, Captain Cook, Diderot, Samuel Johnson, John Ruskin, Darwin, Dickens and many other notables are examined, much of it obsolete for a people stepping into the 21st century. For his own part, Elwin argued that India will be best advised to follow a middle path between a policy of 'leave them alone' and one of de-tribalisation. Beyond this there was nothing, no reading material or study, on the people of the North East until the 1980s. Though Nagaland is a State within India, various groups of insurgent Nagas have been disrupting peace in the North Eastern States frequently for the last seventy years. Peace attempts have been made since the 1990s, but it is only in August 2015 that a treaty has been chalked by the Indian state and the major insurgent group for, hopefully, a 'lasting peace' in the region.

mosaic of innumerable tribes and subtribes. It was a vicious cycle of monumental mistakes, errors of judgement and a lack of vision by the government and its officials who were living in the ivory towers of Delhi and Guwahati. All this while, a smiling Chairman Mao was executing his grand design of an armed uprising which would suck major forces of the Eastern Command into the Nagaland and Mizo Hills. It would leave India equally vulnerable along the Chinese border for decades after the 1962 debacle.

Until the turn of the century, India was quite overstretched militarily, thanks to Chinese designs.

This alienation would soon spread and engulf the whole of North East, with China the indirect catalyst. Soon there would be stirrings for a distinct Assamese identity. North East India was hemmed in by West Bengal, (then) East Pakistan and Burma. Northern Burma was totally out of control of Rangoon and China was breathing down India's neck all the while through it. North East was simmering with anger and was gasping for space.

A nation constitutes a people with a defined territory, with a mosaic of shared histories and beliefs. If with such shared destiny, a nation can collectively achieve great dreams, then Nagaland and Mizoram during the 1950s were certainly not part of this process. For them, the issue was separation from India, to be left free to remain a century behind, however impracticable it would be. Good governance and development was the only effective antidote.

Partition or secession was never a solution to ethno-nationalism. There was no option to allow Balkanisation of India any further. Americans chose to go for a civil war in 1861-65, which arose from an attempt by eleven of its southern States to secede from the US.

I remember sitting on a chair in front of a church in a remote Naga village, watching children playing outside among rocks, trees and a flat piece of ground. Suddenly I remembered a sentence I read earlier by Rabindranath Tagore: *From the solemn gloom of the temple, children run out to sit in the dust. God watches them play and forgets the priest.*

In the ultimate analysis, we loved establishing a rapport with the Naga tribes in Tamenglong region, because we loved and respected them. The relationship was born from genuine mutual feelings which grew slowly and steadily and were not based on chicanery, bravado, hoopla and arrogance. It was the magic of small successes, like the sustained momentum of gentle waves, building up slowly and surely towards something bigger.

Truly, counter-insurgency operations can only succeed in the long term if they are built upon the fundamental mantra of winning the hearts and minds of the aggrieved people. Very soon, Pakistan was destined to learn even more bitter lessons than India, when its rampaging Army started wrecking havoc on the aggrieved people of East Pakistan. The People of East Pakistan were demanding their legitimate political space in the Punjabi-dominated West Pakistan-based government and to be treated fairly. A vicious cycle of insurgency and its ruthless suppression was to start soon. The germination of a separate Bengali Muslim nationalism was an embryonic process, the product of which exploded around 1970-1971. Its effects spilled over to India, with over a million refugees escaping the torture and brutal suppression by the Pakistan Army. Thereafter, South Asia would never be the same again. It became a global flash point.

Finally, in Dec 1970, our unit was ordered to move to another field area in Agartala in Tripura, which was a remote hill state of India bordering East Pakistan. A grand tribal farewell party was organised by local Nagas, which again was full of traditional dances, songs, feasting and emotional speeches. A church service was held, which blessed the unit. This tenure was a great experience indeed. By now I had learnt a lot about the sorry plight of the North East. Soldiering in the Indian Army really is a fascinating journey in life. I was deeply in love with my profession.

Meanwhile, a serious insurgency, resulting in a separatist movement was underway in East Pakistan. Pakistan was making much graver mistakes while unleashing its self-empowered military to butcher East Pakistani citizens. A nation masquerading as a democracy was arrogantly digging its own grave. Those who unleash uncontrolled forces should remember that they also unleash uncontrollable counter-forces.

SONAR BANGLA

Crossfire Closer Home

Are you a soldier, compelled by harsh laws of man, to forsake wife and children and go forth into battle for the sake of greed which your leaders miscall duty?

—Khalil Gibran

Such was the predicament of Pakistani soldiers in 1970-1971, when the Pakistani Army was unleashed on their fellow Pakistanis in East Pakistan. Around mid-1971, East Pakistan was on fire. Many Bengali officers of the Pakistan Army, along with some troops who were personnel of the East Pakistan Rifles, as well as young boys from universities in Dhaka and Chittagong, started deserting, crossing over and pouring into the Indian side. East Pakistan was in revolt. The people of East Pakistan wanted independence from Pakistan. Cross-border firings gradually intensified. A war-like situation soon engulfed the region. The deserters reorganised themselves, along with thousands of young boys who had defected into India, and formed the Mukti Bahni or Liberation Army.

Agartala was a picturesque, sleepy, isolated town with a prominent, architecturally beautiful palace of the erstwhile Maharaja of Tripura. The surrounding areas were hilly, jungle-clad up to the international border of East Pakistan. The Gods of War and Destiny were locating the units of my Brigade in an area which was soon to become one of the major launching pads for the looming Indo-Pak war of 1971.

The ensuing battles were to bring glory to the battalion, at the cost of many of its officers and troops who would be killed and wounded. We young officers were not so aware of the shape of things to come. The Commanding Officer knew and a few senior officers had premonition of this.

'The infantry battalion, this infantry battalion, our infantry battalion, the unit in which we are commissioned, is the moral symbol of our military lives', said the Commanding Officer of our battalion in 1971, Lt Col PC Sawhney.

The terrain of Tripura was ideal for training. The battalion, as part of the Brigade, got busy training for conventional warfare which was totally different from counter-insurgency operations, in which the unit was engaged for the last two years in the Naga Hills. It was back to basics of tactics, fire and move, attack, defence, bunker bursting, infiltration into enemy terrain, raids etc.

During lulls in training, officers played basketball, volleyball, hockey, football with the troops amidst intense competition and enthusiasm. Officers' team versus non-commissioned officers' teams, inter-rifle companies competitions, competitions with neighbouring infantry battalions, which were rather intense. Along with me, young officers like Ravi, Mohan Lal, Sunil Subandh, KC Sharma, KD Singh, the new Second Lieutenant Mazumdar and Choudhary were active players.

While in Manipur, Nagaland, all officers were deployed in various outlying posts and never together. Now was a period of good regimental routine, with great interaction between all officers and troops. Years later, I would reflect upon this period as destiny preparing the unit for the historic, fierce battles that lay ahead.

The young officers of the unit became popular with the local girls at Agartala, who were well-educated and from good families. The Commanding Officer and some senior Majors were always a bit apprehensive on this score. They lectured these officers about chivalry and the need to treat such ladies with dignity and propriety.

Some of these young ladies, along with their parents at times, were invited to watch some sports competitions. Young officers were keen to impress them with their sporting skills, though the accompanying parents were never looked forward to.

One day, Captain Ravi and I managed to hitch a helicopter flight, with the help of an Air Force pilot who was my friend at the RIMC. It was a routine training flight. I had requested the Rimcollean pilot to fly over a part of Agartala, so that I could locate the house of a very talented, graceful girl. I had asked the girl to stand on the roof of her house at a specified time. I did not tell her about the helicopter. It was a well-planned act. The helicopter hovered a while over an area I indicated. After a while I could see the girl on the roof of the house. As the helicopter flew low over the house and hovered a while, I threw a bunch of flowers towards the girl which missed the roof and fell on her father's head in the garden below.

The Commanding Officer, on hearing about this escapade, was not amused. Ravi and I were formally marched up to his office and reprimanded. The charge was, 'Misuse of official hardware (helicopter) to woo a girl'. Later, Mohan Lal joked, saying, 'Sir, thank God you used only official hardware to woo a girl!'.

By November 1971, war became imminent as by then millions of civilians had poured into India from East Pakistan to escape extreme brutalities inflicted on them by the rampaging Pakistan Army. Agartala town was only a couple of miles from the international border. The people of Agartala were told to dig in around their houses as artillery shelling was imminent. The sleepy town of Agartala was rudely awakened to the implications of war. Army units moved into battle locations along the border. Soon, for the first time, the people of Agartala would see its Army fighting and dying, getting wounded in large numbers. This was no skirmishes with our own people, it was war with another country.

The Brigade had the first task of capturing Akhaura, an important railhead in East Pakistan, close to the border. The battle of Akhaura was a tough operation. Akhaura was captured, but with heavy casualties. The Brigade had three excellent battalions with a fine artillery unit. The Brigade Commander was a spirited, courageous Brigadier. Lt Colonel Sawhney was an inspirational Commanding Officer. During this battle, Major Mauji, Major DP Singh, Captain MM Ravi, Captain KC Katoch, Captain KS Narang, Captain Sunil Subandh, Captain KD Singh were wounded and evacuated by Air Force helicopters. Captain KC Sharma, Second Lieutenant KK Mazumdar and Lieutenant MPS Chaudhary were killed. Forty-six jawans died and 127 were wounded, five JCOs were killed. Other two infantry battalions also suffered casualties.

Victory in battle always comes at a heavy cost. After the war, nations celebrate the victory, but usually forget the brave who died. Most third world countries display such tendencies.

After the capture of Akhaura, it was a continuous speedy series of operations. Speed was essential to avoid future heavy casualties by not allowing the enemy to regroup. Speed was also possible because the enormous amount of local support and the help rendered by the Mukti Bahini. Whenever the enemy destroyed bridges over various rivers, helicopters would lift some units across. On the other side, thousands of Bengalis of East Pakistan would cheer the Indian Army and ferry the heavy equipment to the nearest road. Hundreds of rickshaws, and the few local transport would take the troops to close in with the retreating enemy. It was all an amazing experience.

Some reinforcement in term of officers and troops soon started joining the battalions to replenish their depleted strengths. The only Lieutenant who was alive and kicking was Lt Mohan Lal, who later lamented, '*Ek bhi saali goli mujh par nahi lagi. Kam se kam ek taang men hi lag jati to mujhe* wound medal *milta.* (Not one f…ing bullet hit me. At least if one bullet would have hit my leg, I would have got a wound medal.)'

Any clash between the Indian and the Pakistan Army is a serious clash between two professional, well-trained and motivated forces. Whenever an engagement takes place, both sides fight bravely with no holds barred. This was so, in the initial seven to ten days of the Bangladesh war. Soon, the enemy (Pakistani Army) realised the grimness of the situation and the fact that local support was intense for the Indian Army and the accompanying Mukti Bahini. The brutal suppression of the people of East Pakistan had cost the Pak Army too much. Most of the locals, who had earlier collaborated with the Pakistan Army, deserted them, to avoid punishment. No one had expected such a situation.

The Pak Army's withdrawal to Dhaka was chaotic; with many officers abandoning their troops and retreating to Dhaka. Soon, surrenders by Pakistan Army units and their scattered, virtually un-led elements started. They were treated well by the Indian Army. Some remaining troops, who had lost contact with their units and could not formally surrender were caught by rampaging, frenzied mobs who lynched and slaughtered them rather viciously. The pent up feelings from experiences of the brutalities and humiliation inflicted on Bengali Pakistanis by the Pakistan Army exploded and whenever they managed to catch stray soldiers, as well as known collaborators, the punishment meted out was swift and merciless. Abandonment of troops by many officers in the East Pakistan sector was indeed intriguing. Such an aberration could only happen due to the resulting panic in an occupation army, which was bereft of any government control and civilian support, wherein officers let down their troops during a defeat.

To be fair, there were some Pakistani officers who bravely remained with their troops and had inflicted losses on the Indian Army till the end. There were also many good officers, who stuck with their troops and surrendered only to avoid needless loss of lives, thanks to a no-win situation. Such officers belonged to excellent units of the Pakistan Army and which were placed in very adverse situations by bad Generals. Generalship in the Pakistan Army had certainly degenerated to its lowest levels ever in 1970. However, when it came to the treatment of prisoners of war, the Indian Army was clearly more chivalrous and more abiding by the spirit of the Geneva Convention. Certainly, the impact of grooming under the British and adopting their traditions and ethos was one reason for the model behaviour of the Indians. The Pakistani officers too had inherited the same British grooming and traditions but the excellent junior officers could do little when their Generals had become corrupt.

A strange experience during this period of conflict will forever be etched in my mind and soul. On 14 December 1971, my battalion was marching towards Dhaka, which was about fifteen kilometres away. All this was possible due to a series of furious battles fought since 3rd December. During these battles, no quarters were given by the Indian and Pakistani military forces. The initial battles to penetrate the stubborn defences of the Pakistan Army were won at the cost of heavy casualties. Thereafter, the support provided by Mukti Bahini and people of East Pakistan was so intense that the fortitude of the Pakistani Army cracked. My battalion suffered heavy casualties. Incredible courage and daring was displayed by the officers and the men. Our commanding officer, Colonel Sawhney displayed great leadership.

I, then an Adjutant, was moving with a detachment of about twenty soldiers through a village. Some cheering locals directed us towards the nearby highway. Scores of rickshaws, tractors, trolleys and some dilapidated buses were waiting to take us quickly towards the withdrawing Pakistanis.

In a part of the village, a mob of about hundred had six Pakistani soldiers among them. Four of the hapless soldiers were clobbered to death. Two soldiers were tied up on a tree, awaiting their turn. I fired my weapon in the air, yelling in Bengali to stop the carnage. The crowd would not stop. Some villagers tried to explain how these soldiers and their units had raped, murdered and tortured civilians during the last one year. 'Now they want to surrender and live after being defeated. These bullies, cowards, killers and rapists of fellow Muslims deserve death', they said.

I told my troops to quickly untie and take charge of the two soldiers, which was promptly done. The villagers protested and started demanding that the two soldiers should be handed over to them. One soldier was wearing a black dungaree. He was from a tank unit. He was mumbling his prayers and was admirably calm. I asked the soldier to tell us what had happened, how he felt. The soldier mumbled that his time to answer to Allah had come, for the acts of atrocities on fellow Muslims. So he was praying to Allah to give him the courage to face the consequences.

The other soldier was from a Baloch Regiment. His eyes were closed as if he was drugged. When I asked him, he said, 'Yes, we did *Gunah* (sin), on our own people. But sir, I did not kill fellow Muslims deliberately. I mistook some to be *Kafirs* (non-Muslims), based on wrong information from unit sources. Now I have to die.'

I told both of them, 'you will not die. Had we arrived a few minutes earlier, we would not have let the other four die. You both are prisoners of the Indian Army now.' By now, a column of our own troops became visible nearby. The villagers, after having butchered the four soldiers, their anger abated a bit, realised that these two Pakistani soldiers could not be killed and grudgingly started moving away, shouting, 'Joy Bangla, death to Punjabis and collaborators'. The term 'Punjabi' signified the Pakistan Army. In the eyes of the people of East Pakistan, the Army was mainly Punjabi. All others were peripheral parts of that Army.

As Indian Army units were marching towards Dhaka, the Pakistani Army in East Pakistan formally surrendered. On our way, I initiated a conversation with the rescued prisoner from the Baloch Regiment. He was a man named Naik Ali.

'So Ali, your Baluch Regiment fought well', I stated.

'Sahib', replied Ali. 'We Balochis are good fighters. But in Pakistan Army, the Punjabis dominate. They get most of the credit and enjoy more powers. Punjabis are richer as they possess most of the fertile land. We are sidelings.'

'Why so?' I encouraged him to speak up.

'Sahib, in Pakistan, the Punjabis discriminate against Balochis, Bengalis, Pathans, Sindhis, Biharis, tribals and all others. Sindhis hate Punjabis, Biharis, Balochis and the rest. Similarly, we Balochis are not comfortable with Sindhis, Biharis and Pathans, but we dislike the arrogant Punjabis the most. We want to belong to Pakistan but always suffer from a feeling of discrimination.'

'Now I realise how lucky the Bengalis are', continued Ali after a pause. 'They have suffered so much, but they really resisted. Now they have their own country. Geography helped them. That is why India could help them so much. We Balochis would also want to have our own country. But India will never be able to help us like they helped the Bengalis. We will also never have a leader like Shiekh Majibur. Sahib, I am saying all this to you because you saved us from a horrible death.'

'Don't worry Ali. You will soon go home', I said encouragingly. 'Now, can you explain to me one thing which troubles me about you all? How have you convinced your own mind and soul that killing non-Muslim civilians was justified, but killing fellow Muslims was a gunah?'

Naik Ali kept quiet. While handing over the two rescued Pakistani soldiers as prisoners of war, I told them both, 'You both are brave but misguided soldiers. When you go home, do tell everybody about this experience truthfully.'

Soon a very interesting and fascinating situation developed. Nearly 90,000 Pakistani soldiers had formally surrendered, with weapons and huge military hardware. Thousands of them were billeted as prisoners in Dhaka Cantonment barracks, duly barricaded, fenced and heavily guarded by Indian Army units. The Bihari Muslims of East Pakistan, who had collaborated with the Pakistan Army, were also targets of public wrath. They too were protected by Indian Army units. They all volunteered to be repatriated to Pakistan and join the Mohajirs there. 'Mohajirs' were those Muslims from the hinterland of India, mostly from Bihar, who had opted to be a part of Pakistan during partition. Pakistan had refused to accept them after 1971.

Later on, as I reflected on this experience of the 1971 war, I realised that excellent soldiers existed in the armed forces of both India and Pakistan. Both are amongst the best in the world. The difference is in the methods used for motivating the respective military forces. Indian military ethos is based on romantic patriotism towards the motherland, regimental pride, ie *izzat* and the protection of the democratic system. It is certainly not religious per se. Role of religion is restricted to praying to God for victory, invoking blessings and divine protection. Indian military leadership never indulged in misleading its troops by wrong interpretation of religion. This, perhaps, is the most critical aspect of India's national security, which has not been fully appreciated in India or by those who run India.

God help India if it violates this military ethos ever, notwithstanding severe provocations to the contrary, from its neighbourhood.

I gathered these impressions from my understanding of officers and men of the Pakistan Army during the 1971 war and the interactions with many of them as prisoners of war at Dhaka.

I felt very proud of my country and the armed forces. Though the Pakistan Army officers were professionally competent and brave, they always gave the impression of arrogance while dealing with the troops. Indian Army jawans respected their officers while Pakistan Army jawans feared their officers. This dynamics is curiously true at the national level as well, in the two respective countries. While Indian Armed Forces are respected in Indian society, Pakistan Armed Force are mostly feared by the Pakistani society as well as the Pakistani government. While the Indian Army serves India, the Pakistani Army actually rules Pakistan.

Another observation of mine was a rather troublesome one. The intensity of repression committed by the professional Pakistan Army on the citizens in East Pakistan was unbelievable. Obviously, civilian control over the Army was completely missing. The highest military leadership in Pakistan at that point of time was very bad indeed. I did feel that, however much one criticised Indian politicians and bureaucrats, Indian democracy was the best thing for India. In any healthy society, civilian control of the military is a key factor and more so, the Indian Armed Forces are comfortable with this system.

No country can be allowed to let loose the military on its own people with such gay abandon. Such a policy will inevitably result in local uprisings, causing uncontrolled spurts of insurgency. The intensity of East Pakistan's hatred towards Pakistan, which was built up over a period of time due to grave injustices and atrocities perpetuated on them, was also unbelievable. Seeing this, I really hoped that an emerging India would provide leadership for the future prosperity and coexistence of a democratic South Asia.

Such were the thoughts and hopes of a young army officer. I was unaware at the time of the complexities of politics, and the internal and external realities of games that nations play in a complex world.

India's sheer size, its democratic roots and its critical role in South Asia would inevitably lead to its involvement in any serious insurgency warfare in its neighbouring countries. India's expertise in tackling insurgency, either home grown or in its neighbourhood, would always be tested from time to time. In fact, in the coming decades, insurgency would assume state sponsorship by antagonistic neighbours in order to weaken India and would be a part of their strategy. India was perhaps destined to live with insurgency, whether home grown due to weak internal governance or foreign sponsored.

A decade or two after the 1971 war, which started with the insurgency in East Pakistan, the nature of war between nations would change very substantially. Henceforth, every use of the Indian Army for meeting threats to national security would be linked to insurgency. The 1971 war itself showed the shape of things to come. Even the 1948 Indo-Pakistan conflict in Kashmir was conducted in the guise of insurgents and militias. The linkage between lack of good governance and internal security was manifest, whether in India or in its neighbourhood, and would affect the Indian Army. Third world nations like India generally has a third rate police force, which further makes things worse and even more unmanageable.

When history is truly made but converted into a false scripture and turn some selected persons into deities, truth becomes the final casualty. Such a nation misses out on the long-term benefits of a great victory.

After the liberation of Bangladesh, our battalion settled down at the small cantonment of Kanchrapara, near Calcutta. The Headquarters of Eastern Command at Calcutta's Fort William, which had conducted the entire war in the Eastern Sector, wanted to celebrate the Independence Day Parade in a grand manner in August 1972. Our battalion camped outside Fort William and was given various responsibilities for the conduct of the parade. Captain Ravi, Captain Julius Toppno, Major Devinder, Major Mauji, Major Katoch had re-joined the unit after being treated for their battle wounds at various military hospitals. They were the pride of the unit. They wore their war medals with pride.

The officers decided to have dinner on a Saturday evening at the Officers Club in Fort William.

'Ram Bachan, chilled beer *hai?* (Ram Bachan, do you have some chilled beer for us?)', Ravi asked the barman.

'*Bilkul chilli hai sahib* (it is really chilled)', said Ram Bachan.

The officers settled down for the beer session, which invariably implied long, loud discussions on various subjects, full of the choicest of adjectives to drive home their opinions.

'After such a victory, India will become a big power within the next two decades. This is a period of great opportunity for the country. India should think big now', I said, the perpetual dreamer. 'Cheers to that.'

'*Ghanta* (bullshit). Nothing of that sort will happen', laughed Mohan Lal. 'You don't know about our short-sighted politicians and the arrogant, know-all bureaucrats. I am from Delhi and I know what I am saying.'

'Mohan Lal', said Mauji. 'He may be right. India's self-esteem has been aroused. We have sorted out Pakistan and helped to create a new nation of Bangladesh. We took 90,000 prisoners of war, which is historic. There can never be a better time than this for India to launch itself forward. The morale of the people is very high.'

'Sir, politics is all about staying in power. For the foreseeable future, this has been assured due to our military victory. Political vision is limited to the next elections', retorted Mohan Lal.

'They don't care a f..k about Mother India. The bastards have returned 90,000 prisoners of war without taking our soldiers and officers back, who were captured and shipped off to West Pakistan. Some of our troops were captured in the Western Sector. They too are still there. The government has let down its Armed Forces. It will do so again and again.'

'Ram Bachan, chicken tikka and kajus please', said Ravi. He preferred to drink beer straight from the bottle rather fast in true Coorg style. 'Yaar, when I see the nation depicting our victory in magazines, newspapers and calendars via photographs of our Prime Minister, personified as Goddess Durga slaying her enemies, I feel very angry. Okay, she was a bold, decisive Prime Minister and deserves praise but this sort of *chamchagiri* or sycophancy by the people is a shame.'

Captain Julius tried to temper the discussion and exclaimed, 'Relax, relax. Such things happen in the corridors of power. Indian democracy provides less space for the military institutions and we should take such things lightly. The people of India have great admiration for the Armed Forces.'

I quite agreed with Ravi. I sighed, 'Our national leaders and civil services do not display much penchant to honour the Armed Forces, except in a superficial manner. They are too arrogant, egoistical and conceited. They just don't want to perpetuate the glory achieved by military forces, beyond a point. A nation which does not recognise its soldiers, can never become a big power in the world stage. It may do well somewhat, but can never become a great power. The History of nations proves this.'

Major Devinder, in the initial stages of the discussion, was busy eyeing and savouring the figures of some attractive ladies who were in the club. He now joined in, 'Gentlemen, see the British, Americans and Europeans, how they honour their military forces. They made legends out of Generals Patton, Slim, Montgomery, Auchinleck, Rommel, Manstein etc. They were all national heroes and acknowledged by the governments and the entire nation. They also acknowledged the leadership of Prime Minister Winston Churchill as well as the resolve of the British citizens, braving the attacks on London. Look at the National War Memorials of such nations, built and maintained with poignant pride, grace and gratitude. See our India Gate which is like a cheap picnic spot. We are bloody *besharams* (shameless).'

'Listen, you youngsters', stated Mauji Ram. 'I am older to you all and I am a Jat; hence more practical than emotional. I was born seven years before independence. The slogan was *Freedom is our Right*, which was true. But it was equally true that freedom must be very well deserved, hard won and really fought for. Freedom should not descend to a people due to prevailing global compulsions rather than for other reasons. A people must raise themselves and earn freedom as a well-deserved blessing, before it can be enjoyed. Then only freedom will have value. Countries and civilisations which take freedom for granted for too long, are finally taught a lesson by history and eventually suffer from leadership deficit. So, do not expect too much from those who govern the country. The 1971 war will never be forgotten by Pakistan but India will forget it soon. Mark my words. India has quite forgotten the 1962 defeat from China. If it hadn't, then we would have taken greater care of the North East border and our preparedness against China would have been better than it is, by now.'

'*Sirji*, that is what I am trying to say, but *sala* juniors are never given a proper hearing', lamented Mohan Lal. Everyone burst out laughing. 'We Indians are good at petty politics and tactics relating to small issues. Geoeconomics, Geopolitics and Geostrategy have been our Achilles' heels for five thousand years. Believe me: we will fail to live up to the high pedestal that we have set in 1971. We will pat ourselves for a great victory, remain satisfied with short-term gains which have been made and miss out on the larger issues. This will be the situation, till we get a kick on our arse.'

During the entire discussion, Katoch had quietly polished off two bottles of beer. This was the minimum he required, before he too became a thinker and gave some solemn advice. He raised one finger. Julius promptly said, 'Katoch Sir, the toilet is on the left of the corridor.'

'Shut up Julius', said Katoch amidst another burst of laughter from the others. 'I was raising my hand to get a chance to speak.'

'Gentlemen, you all are apprehensive that India will miss all opportunities to become a great nation. Judging by the conduct of all you guys so far this evening, I am convinced that it will. Four very beautiful ladies are in the club this evening. One has been blessed by God with beautiful breasts, one has a waist which can launch a thousand ships, one has eyes which have the *nasha* of the best scotch whisky in the world and one has a *makkhan*-type of complexion, smooth as Kanjivaram silk. All of you have missed the opportunity to inspect them except Devinder and me. Even if we could not do so physically, we did them mentally. To avail of any opportunity, you have to develop a knack of being an opportunist and never miss opportunities. See the basic point?'

'Que Sera Sera, what will be, will be', I sang. 'For now, let us celebrate the fact that we all experienced a great event in our military career. Let us all refill our beer jugs and drink in the memory of the officers and the men from our unit who died in combat.'

'One only wishes that there is a system wherein officers of the civil services, particularly the Indian Administrative Service and the Indian Foreign Service, interact with us and understand our way of life and how we feel. They would then understand how we experience and perceive things. Such interactions would help us to correct our perceptions. We have so much to tell each other and understand from each other. We may then feel more positive about the nation and its developmental processes', sighed Ravi.

'*Ghanta*', laughed Mohan Lal aloud. 'Nothing like that will happen. None of them are interested in any interaction. India is their *jagir* (property) and we are nothing.'

'Okay Mohan', smiled Mauji, 'you have finished your quota of *ghantas*. Your *ghanta* philosophy will make us very cynical about them, which is not a good thing.'

An elderly, retired officer was sitting nearby. He walked up and said, 'Gentlemen, I am Colonel Agnihotri. I retired from the Army in 1968. I was an instructor of General Manekshaw, when he did the Senior Officers' Course.'

All the unit officers got up and shook hands with the veteran senior officer. 'Please join us for a drink sir', said Mauji.

'Thanks friends, I occasionally come to the club. I drink two small pegs of whisky. When I watch the unit officers that come here, hear them and see their *josh* and high spirits, I feel very good. I have been listening a bit to you all. I have had my permissible quota of two small pegs. May I wrap up the evening with a few concluding remarks, on all that you people discussed?'

'We will be honoured Sir', replied Mauji.

'Basically, third world countries are like cockroaches, one pulling down the other', grinned Colonel Agnihotri. 'I feel this will happen now. We are unlikely to be able to digest such a magnitude of success as a nation. Now our own people who govern us will let each other down.'

'Why Sir?' I asked.

'We simply can't digest this victory, because historically and culturally, we suffer from serious fault lines. I see Pakistan bouncing back again as a determined, angry and vengeful nation with a single point agenda of taking revenge on India at all costs. We shall have to bear the cost of this military victory in the coming decades. I don't mean to say we should be afraid of future threats from Pakistan. We should prepare ourselves for greater threats. In our euphoria of this victory, our politicians will fail to galvanise our nation.

'I have another fear. Our victory in the 1971 war will make us forget our defeat of 1962. This would be a serious blunder. This will happen. The government of India, in any case, will forget the 1962 defeat. This will be because the 1962 defeat was a defeat of the political and bureaucratic leadership primarily. They let down the nation and the Armed Forces. My fear is that the Indian Armed Forces will also tend to do the same in due course of time. While the civilian government in Pakistan may tend to forget the 1971 defeat after a few decades, the Pakistan Armed Forces will never forget it. This will be a crucial difference. We better watch out for China. We are under their intense observation. China will try to *Bonsai* India. One of you rightly used the terms Geopolitics and Geostrategy. The only think-tank available, which advises the government, is the IAS and IFS bureaucrats. While they are very bright indeed at the entry level, their intellectual growth thereafter is very limited, due to their arrogance of power and ignorance on larger strategic issues, a fact which they will never accept. Their ability to speak big English will, of course, increase a lot.

'1971 was basically a military victory under a very capable Prime Minister indeed. I feel that a country, which never thought through such a massive victory at the outset, can't take full advantage of it. Indo-Pak rivalry will never end till India becomes the most powerful nation in Asia. That is not likely to happen.

'Imagine if, due to political pressure of the government in accordance with bureaucratic advice, Manekshaw had agreed to launch the war six to eight months earlier? Before the groundwork had been done and the Pakistani forces softened by the infiltration of India-trained Bangladeshi guerrillas. The results would not have been so spectacular. I wonder if in the future, we will have Army Chiefs who have such solid balls as Manekshaw. In fact, the future governments may never appoint a soldier and officer like him as Chief, even if we did have a person of his calibre and charisma again.'

'In fact', pontificated Colonel Agnihotri, 'a few years from now, say by mid-1970s onwards, idealism and greatness will walk out of Indian politics and fade away into the sunset for quite a while. Another critical lesson from the 1971 war that we should not fail to take is that, when any nation ignores the development and legitimate aspirations of a large segment of its population, it will crack up. Revolutionary ideas will germinates in the hearts and minds of such a segment of the nation. When that festers for a long time, they take up arms against their own government. The East Pakistanis turned into Bangladeshis in a similar fashion. We in India must never do the same to our own citizens, in any part of the country. Please forgive an old retired Colonel for barging in and doing a summing up of an excellent discussion you people were engaging in. Keep the flag flying friends. Good night to you all.'

The old veteran left the club. He was walking with a discernible limp. Col Agnihotri had been severely wounded in the 1962 war.

Mauji directed me to see him off out of the club. On reaching the car park, I asked, 'Sir, at this stage, what are your views about your military life? Anything you would like to advise me about?'

'Aah!' exclaimed the grand old man. 'What do I tell you? Your generation of officers are smarter, more aware and much more ambitious. Never let down your troops and subordinate officers. Respect and impress your superiors by hard work and character, but never become a bloody sycophant. If you don't get to serve under a superior whom you respect, you do your best and let him go and f..k himself. Whenever your unit does well, and you get compliments from your superiors, tell them that it was all due to your troop's hard work. Whenever there is a f…up, take the blame on yourself, like a soldier, officer and gentleman.'

'And remember lad', continued Col Agnihotri, 'promotions in the Armed Forces is the steepest pyramid amongst all other central government services. So while you should be ambitious to get into the senior ranks, never take an unfair, unethical approach towards promotions.'

'And Sir, your final words about your life', I persisted, realising that the old man needed to go.

'Well, finally, I can tell you that I have the finest woman as my wife, our two children are all doing extremely well in life and we have excellent grandchildren. I have lived an honourable, high-quality and an adventurous life. I have faced death very closely indeed. I have seen my brave troops and officers dying valiantly. My retired life has also been great. I am not rich by civilian standards but am reasonably comfortable. I couldn't have demanded anything more from God. I can only thank him again and again. It has been a well lived life indeed.'

SRI LANKA

Treading on Tamil Toes

Not even the best counter-insurgency techniques make much difference, because neither a foreign occupier nor any puppet government he installs can gain legitimacy.

—Retired US Air Force Colonel Chet Richards, in his book, *If We Can Keep It: A National Security Manifesto for the Next Administration*

Consider the name 'The Liberation Tigers of Tamil Eelam' (LTTE). Tigers and Eelam (independent nation) were empowering words and depicted a clear identity. In contrast, Indian Peace Keeping Force (IPKF) was a confusing and deceptively placid term. The term IPKF depicted a very puerile vision. What ironical use of terms! How much the usage of these two terminologies revealed!

During the period 1987-89, I was the Commanding Officer of an Infantry Battalion of my Regiment. Counter-insurgency operations in a neighbouring country was far from our minds. The situation in Sri Lanka was grim and extremely messy. There were too many questions and not enough answers. The LTTE was a professional insurgent organisation, which was in conflict with Sri Lanka and was fighting a deadly war within its own country. Their agenda was to secede from Sri Lanka and form a separate country in specified northern and north eastern parts where Sri Lankan Tamils were in majority.

A fair degree of moral support existed for them in the State of Tamil Nadu in India, located across the Gulf of Mannar and Palk Strait. The LTTE had several suicide squads who would blow themselves up in busy urban centres of Sri Lanka, causing massive casualties to civilians. Sri Lankan Armed Forces and police would respond with equal violence, against both, its Tamil people and the insurgents. The LTTE was capable of taking on the regular military forces and heavy casualties were inflicted. With the rise of the LTTE in the 1980s, terrorism was born in South Asia.

After a series of complex military and political developments, India and Sri Lanka entered into a Treaty in which the Indian Army would enter Sri Lanka for operations which would lead to the surrender of the LTTE as a prelude to peace talks. The peace talks should then help in setting the negotiating terms, wherein the rights of Tamils to govern themselves would be guaranteed within the framework of the constitution of Sri Lanka. This much was known to us in broad terms.

I was busy training my battalion for a forthcoming major exercise with troops, for conventional operations in the high-altitude regions of India's North East, when I received formal orders to move along with the 9th Battalion, the Bihar Regiment, to Sri Lanka in the Trincomalee sector. The change was considerable; from High-altitude Mountain Warfare training in the Himalayas to the coastal and humid jungles of North East Sri Lanka for live operations. The battalion was neither equipped nor trained for such a major operational reorientation. Unlike in Bangladesh, it had no local support. Unlike in Bangladesh, our mission was not liberation of an oppressed people.

The move was to be immediate. It appeared to a perplexed Commanding Officer and a newly-promoted Colonel, with twenty years of service, that neither the political leadership nor the powerful bureaucrats at the MoD had changed much since 1962. Twenty-five years after the 1962 defeat, they would still not hesitate to order the military in such a thoughtless and unprofessional manner. It was akin to the Home Ministry ordering a hundred companies of the Central Police Forces for deployment towards election duty in Bihar or Kerala. It seemed as simple as that to them, perhaps. Probably this was how troops, elephants and horses were mobilised and hurriedly sent to Panipat, to fight the battle to save India from the invading forces of Babar in 1526.

India and strategic insight appeared to be parallel lines, never seeming to meet.

I realised that as a Commanding Officer, I could ill-afford to display my confusions and concerns to my officers and men. I, however, realised that the Ministry of Defence (MOD) in India was ill-equipped to handle serious issues relating to correct and judicious application of military power to achieve critical national interests. I also felt that the military hierarchy was not empowered enough to stand up and be counted in such situations. I set about to handle my dilemmas of commanding troops in battle amidst such ambiguity. I wrote a small letter to my family Guru in Calcutta, seeking his blessings and prayers for my troops.

As my battalion embarked on a merchant ship hired to take us from Madras port to Trincomalee, I felt butterflies in my stomach. The input given to me about Sri Lanka, its terrain, its people, the ground situation etc were very scanty. There were no maps, poor quality air photographs as well as unconvincing details of the LTTE relating to their actual strength, their organisation, their resolve to fight, how they operated. Even the assurances that they were ready to surrender to the IPKF were unconvincing. There were no clear tasks specified and aims to be achieved spelt out. Clearly, it was a case of authority exercised by the civilian government and responsibility assigned to the Army, to achieve vague objectives in whatever situation they would encounter in a foreign country.

In fact, the Indian Army should have demanded a strategic debate and discussion with the politicians, before being sent out to Sri Lanka. They should have asked for clear tasks, an intelligence summary, specified national objectives, specified end results and enhanced capabilities to handle the situation. An incredulous situation indeed! I adopted a stoic stance. I was in a critical professional situation, as were all other Commanding Officers, at that particular time in Sri Lanka.

As I watched my men disembarking and unloading equipment, stores and vehicles at Trincomalee port, I tried to hide my trepidation by regularly chatting up with the troops and encouraging them by saying things like, '*Shabash, Tagre Raho, Zindgi mein aisa mauka kabhi nahi milega, padosi mulk ko madad karna hamari duty hai*', etc. (Well done, keep your morale high, perk up, this is going to be a rare experience of our lives, our duty is to help a neighbouring country in trouble etc.) While saying all these things, I realised I was not being truthful to them. I felt quite alone for the first time in life, despite being among my men.

Military operations involve lives of men under command. Between officers and men there is a code of conduct. Loss of lives and limbs for a clearly spelt out, worthwhile, defined and understandable objective which was of critical national importance was acceptable. Soldiers believe that otherwise, their officers would not waste their lives as well as their own. Military operations should be based on clear aims and objectives, with the design of battle commensurate with resources that are provided. War is a deadly affair. In a democracy, battles should not be fought for unprincipled or Machiavellian reasons or for sheer malevolence.

Democracy should give adequate space to the top military leadership to stand up, question and demand clear directions which are based on adequate time to prepare and equip forces, before despatching them to uncharted situations. While expecting thousands to sacrifice their lives and limbs, a few military leaders should be prepared to risk their future promotions, if needed.

The first lot of IPKF contingents were told that their purpose was to organise and encourage safe surrender of the LTTE, along with their weapons, as a prelude to a political settlement. They were told that the LTTE had refused to surrender to the Sri Lankan Army. What they encountered on arrival was fierce resistance by the LTTE, which caused heavy casualties.

Later on, to say that that the LTTE reneged on their promise, was not good enough and was not excusable. Initial contingents, who were hurriedly rushed into Sri Lanka, were not fully equipped or organised for such severe fighting. They were not even prepared for any conflict with the LTTE, let alone a deadly conflict. It was understood, the surrender had been politically arranged through the terms of a Treaty. What we found instead was that, in terms of personal weapons, LTTE soldiers were better armed than the Indian Army soldiers. Local support for LTTE was total and deeply rooted. The writ of Colombo was non-existent in the rural North and the North Eastern part of Sri Lanka.

This was the situation under which the Indian Army was hurriedly inducted into Sri Lanka, fifteen years after the 1971 war. Now there was no Manekshaw to resist such unprofessional misuse of the Army. I received a letter from the family Guru from Calcutta.

'Remember my son, in life you are only a participant in some major events. You are neither responsible for creating such events, nor are you part of their solution. Do not brood too much on judging the events. Experience them and learn lessons from them. Such events should not make you a prisoner of your past, decades later. You are facing such an event now. Therefore, always try to find the best you can do in such situations. You are in the military profession, where soldiers under your command willingly pay the ultimate sacrifice. They depend on you and have faith that you will ensure that their lives are sacrificed for very worthwhile cause. Never betray that faith. This is my direction to you. There will always be situations when self doubt and confusion will overwhelm you. Even Krishna could not fully convince Arjuna during the epic battle in Kurukshetra. Finally, Arjuna was resigned to the fact that he was part of an event, which had to happen.'

'I as a religious man, have forsaken worldly responsibility', continued the humble Guru. 'I am in some sense an escapist. I, like any other teacher and guide, can teach you to the best of my abilities. You, however, are not an escapist. Your life is tougher, more purposeful and more prone to struggle than mine. I can pray for you. I am no God. But I pray that God always be with you. Keep in touch with God through prayers. Communicate with HIM as a child does with his mother. There is no scripture which can adequately describe God. He has to be self realised. To Thine Own Self Be True. Never fear. As long as you live your life dutifully and meaningfully, that should be enough. There is no real excellence in all these worldly affairs which can be separated from right living. In the final analysis, life is a summary of some key moments. To live a life well, one must live these key moments with purpose and goodness.'

The battle-hardened but battle-fatigued Sri Lankan Army was not supposed to launch military operations, except in self-defence when attacked. The IPKF had to launch all offensive operations against the Tamil Tigers, who were ethnically of Indian origin. The IPKF had no knowledge of the terrain, local languages or any local intelligence. What an ironical, monstrous Treaty had been formulated by the political leadership of both the countries, in an effort to solve a problem of their own making.

It was a state of utter pandemonium. IPKF was subjected to harsh invectives from Sri Lankans, Tamils as well as from the local media in Tamil Nadu.The situation was too grim to be described as a comedy of errors. 'A tragedy of grave errors and obduracy' was the most apt description of the situation in this Buddhist country, where even their Lord Buddha was from India. The majority Sinhala population were historically migrants from Bengal and Odisha in India.

I and my Battalion forged good professional and personal relations with the Sri Lankan Army units located in our area of responsibility. The Sri Lanka Army was a professionally competent army, which was also launched hurriedly into the conflict, by their government and bureaucrats after years of grave mishandling of a sensitive and explosive situation.

The entire region of South Asia today bears the stigma of insanity, in committing the same mistakes again and again and expecting different consequences and results. The politicians and bureaucrats in South Asia do this very well, an expensive way of doing nothing much, except explaining all blunders by tiresome, bombastic and perfidious oratory. Indian military involvement in Sri Lanka would later serve as a 'case study' for when and why a country should not go to war in a neighbouring country. 'History has the uncanny penchant to inflict punishment for mistakes committed earlier', reflected Brigadier Patil, a very distinguished professional soldier, during a conversation with his commanding officer at Trincomalee one day.

It was evident that Indian politics and diplomacy in the mid-1980s was at the level of a clever high school debating contest, with arrogant politicians and recalcitrant babus sitting atop Mount Opinion in the North Block of Delhi.

Genuinely great powers enhance their influences beyond the national boundaries through their economic power. The effect of this economic might soon spreads far and wide. As they develop, they need to progressively invest on military hard power. Pragmatic and great powers ensure that this economic and commensurate military reach is never outstretched. There is a culmination point of such reach beyond which it becomes strategically counterproductive. Neither India's economic might nor its military might in the 1980s was evident to anybody in this context.

During one of my visits to the troops in an outlying post, a Havildar asked me, 'Sahib, we all are now in Sri Lanka. Last time in ancient history, Ram came here with his army to fight Raavan. Can you tell us who is our Raavan here?'

I was taken aback, but quite impressed with the excellent manner in which the NCO was asking what exactly their mission was here?

'Beta (son), be absolutely clear about one thing while you are here. Whoever has a rifle, whose barrel points towards you, is your Raavan. Such is the reality here.'

While collectively briefing the troops everywhere, my officers and I explained the ground situation to the troops, as the battalion settled down in their widely dispersed deployment. A challenging task lay ahead in controlling and dominating the given area of responsibility, which implied getting into clashes with LTTE forces that were supported by the local population quite wholeheartedly.

The reality of 1986-1989 phase was that the LTTE was extremely motivated, professionally competent, with intense faith in their cause and ability to achieve their Eelam (independence).

They were ruthless towards themselves, their own people and toward anyone who opposed them. A deep-rooted idealism and associated romanticism with their cause existed.

The harshness of the existing ground realities was not fully grasped by government and Army officials in North and South Blocks of New Delhi. If anyone in such places thought that the LTTE leadership could be bought or misled, they were grievously wrong. The military might of India did not deter them. The Tamils of Sri Lanka had realised that they had no future as a part of Sri Lanka. Prabhakaran, the LTTE Chief, was their Subhash Chandra Bose. They were grievously wrong in their perceptions.

In such a tragedy of errors, excesses are invariably committed by any army. Before the arrival of the IPKF, to further compound the tragedy, the Sri Lankan security forces had gotten sucked into this cesspool of failure of their government. The biggest persecution within any country or religion does not usually take place by acts of foreign enemies, but by their own indigenous people. One would assume that in a democracy, no nation would despatch their military forces in such a fatuous manner, without any knowledge of the nuances of the use of military power correctly and purposefully.

Both the militaries of India and Sri Lanka were imbibed with the concept of democracy and of civil supremacy. In such democracies, the civilian government had the responsibility to nurture and look after the military ethos and the military institutions. They should have refrained from hurting their troops' self pride, morale and loyalty. Equally, they should have developed knowledge and expertise on the correct use of military force to achieve critical national interests. The military is not a fire-fighting tool to extinguish fires internally which are created by thoughtless, petty politics and chicanery.

The military in every country must also make a more sincere effort to forge better interaction with their civilian counterparts. Generally, they consider themselves exclusive and elite and tend to remain aloof and underestimate their civilian counterparts. In order to be able to put up their cases to politicians and bureaucrats, to make them aware of the needs of the military, the military needs to forge good working relationship with the civilian arm of any government.

Instead, they tend to remain cut off in their Army Cantonments and golf courses.

Over sixty years after independence, the Indian military, it seems, has not been able to explain to their civilian counterparts face to face, the need for spelling out clear aims, objectives and commensurate resources as well as time for preparation, training etc before launching the Armed Forces into conflict. The need to make the military top brass part of such decision-making is also important. Communicating mainly on files with babus, who are articulate in file analysis and pushing files to and fro to display their power and control, is futile. The 'Yes Sir, we shall do it' is a good military ethos up to Battalion and Brigade levels. Beyond that, one needs to be more introspective and pragmatic. The nation might care two hoots for human lives, the military should always value the lives of its soldiers. There can be no compromise on this.

In the process of insisting on such legitimate genuine concerns, if the politicians and bureaucrats get annoyed, then that much of career risks have to be taken by the military hierarchy during combat situations, as part of their occupational hazards.

I, however, reflected upon this line of thought more rationally. I said to myself, 'today we are in shit as Battalion Commanders. Tomorrow, when some of us become part of the top Army hierarchy, will we remember all this?' I could not get a clear, honest and positive answer to such a complex question to myself.

Colonel Gurusinghe of the Sri Lankan Army was a spirited Infantry Battalion Commander. His sub-units were holding some posts in my area of responsibility. The Battalion HQ of Col Gurusinghe was at Trincomalee. He had invited me and my officers at the officers mess.

It was an interaction wherein officers of both the battalions could spend an evening together, relax and understand each other. Gurusinghe and I had done the Junior Command Course together in the College of Combat, Mhow in India in 1974. We both realised that there was some discomfiture about the fact that a foreign army was operating in Sri Lanka, when they (the Lankan Army) should have been doing so. But this was a rather mixed feeling because prior to the arrival of the IPKF, the Sri Lankan Army was rather battle-fatigued, having suffered heavy casualties among young officers and men. Both sides had fought each other to a stalemate. A break from active operations would rejuvenate the Sri Lankan Armed Forces and allow them to recoup and reinforce. Perhaps the final battles would have to be fought by them in the future, seeing the reluctance of the LTTE to surrender to them or anyone else. It was not difficult for the IPKF to empathise with the Sri Lanka Army, because both the armies were always friendly to each other. Most of the officers of Sri Lanka Army had been attending various courses in the training institutions of India. Moreover, the IPKF too was in a very awkward situation. It had to fight the Tamils of Sri Lanka, who were in a deadly conflict with the Sri Lanka government for serious perceived injustices and indignities inflicted on them over decades.

I and my officers noticed that several officers and men of the Sri Lankan Battalion were wearing medals awarded for receiving injuries in battles with the LTTE. Many of those who did not wear the wound medals were newly-recruited troops and newly-commissioned officers. However, all ranks looked fit and their spirits were high. The Sri Lankan government was also blessed with professionally competent, fiercely patriotic and loyal Armed Forces.

Soon, as the drinks were served, the bonhomie grew and the usual fauji discussions started. Colonel Gurusinghe offered a toast to the IPKF, wishing it all success in the challenges ahead. I also offered a toast to the Sri Lanka Army and to the future peace and prosperity for the beautiful island nation. The Regimental Band played great tunes in the background. Sri Lankans are great lovers of music and dance. All officers intermingled around the bar, enjoying themselves and sharing each other's jokes, most of which were salacious in nature.

Colonel Gurusinghe and I strolled out of the mess to allow our officers to enjoy themselves. Outside, the sea view was lovely and the breeze was fresh.

Gurusinghe asked, 'We understand the strange predicament we find ourselves in, isn't it Dadu? What a messy situation we are embroiled in! How are my other friends who did the Junior Command Course in 1974?'

I replied, 'Balwinder Singh is commanding an Artillery Regiment in Jhansi. Remember Alfred who used to exclaim 'Duck F…er, all instructors are Duck F…ers!' He is commanding an Armoured Regiment near Jammu. Joshi and Jamwal did not make it to the rank of Colonel. Joshi is doing a good job in a business firm. Jamwal has moved to the USA and is well settled there.'

'Yes, it is indeed a strange predicament we find ourselves in', I continued. 'Your dilemma is dominated by the Sri Lankan flavour, mine by the Indian perspective. We do not have the luxury of analysing the backgrounds of the whys and hows. Here is a complex situation and we have a job to do here, though I cannot make much f…ing sense of what is happening.'

'Friend, in the higher scheme of things, we are small fries. Remember once in Mhow, what Balwinder was singing in the bar?

Hitler had one big ball
Rommel had two but they were small
Himmler had something similar
But Goebells had no balls at all.'

We both laughed out loud. I exclaimed, '*Yaar* Gurusinghe, maybe something is wrong with the testicles of the leaders in this part of the world. Either they have a small one, or one big one and many don't have them at all.'

Now the two Battalion Commanders really felt relaxed, meeting each other so long after 1974. Gurusinghe said, 'my Company Commanders in your area have been instructed to provide all help to your officers and men so that you get familiarised with the terrain, the ground situation, the local population and also the intelligence updates. But we are not allowed to operate against the LTTE, as you know. Be very careful. Your officers and troops must always be vigilant. A small act of carelessness can cause heavy casualties. Remember that the LTTE are watching you very carefully. You all will never be able to identify the LTTE from the common people, except when they are carrying weapons. So a couple of LTTE men with hidden small weapons can literally come very near your troops and you will not realise it. You must insist and demand having some Tamil-speaking soldiers in all your posts. Take care. And don't hesitate to contact me, whenever you need my advice.'

'Thanks Guru. We will be in touch. It was really good of you to invite us. We don't have Tamil-speaking troops in our unit. I wonder if I can get them soon enough.'

'But you must have them yaar. I shall arrange for a few Tamil-speaking soldiers to be located in your posts. By the way, do you see any light through the tunnel regarding a peaceful resolution, during your stay here?'

'Guru, I just can't fathom how this problem can be resolved by anyone else but your country', I exclaimed.

'Friend, let us now go inside and see how our youngsters are enjoying. The buggers are of an age group where they do not worry whether they will survive this crisis. They have faith that their Commanding Officer will see them through the crisis. May God give us both the capability to do so.'

'Amen', I gasped hesitatingly.

The band struck the last waltz. How fast the party was ending! How many of these smart, lively young men would soon die or get wounded in the battles ahead. What a waste of their youth and an excellent human resource.

Whenever there was a confrontation between the IPKF and the LTTE, the fighting was tough and intense. The Tamil Tigers were clever and cunning. They had total cooperation of the local Tamil villagers and tribals. They knew the terrain forwards and backwards. Their leadership was of a very strong fibre. They had better personal weapons, comprising AK 47 rifles, than the Indian Army. They were seemingly fighting with desperation, as if for survival. They felt that they had a cause worth dying for, which was the most fundamental prerequisite for any fighting force. They had to fight inside Sri Lanka and they had to win. They had rejected any other choice. Every soldier would prefer to die rather than get captured. They were among the first suicide fighters after the Second World War.

They were also very angry with India and its representative, the Indian Army. For them, this was a monstrous betrayal. Casualties to both the IPKF and the LTTE were heavy. Some collateral, unintentional damage to civilians was impossible to avoid. In some cases, civilians would give them cover in order to help them escape. In some cases, the LTTE would deliberately use unarmed civilians as cover to hit and escape.

There was no doubt that what was seen as something of strategic importance to the mandarins of the North and South Block in New Delhi, appeared to be senseless and purposeless, even insincere and mad, to the commanders of the troops under fire, on the ground.

We all felt India, as the largest country in South Asia, may have to pay a heavy price in future for being in a neighbouring country under these circumstances. Could India really provide leadership and direction to South Asia in this manner? If not, such a vacuum would get filled by some other power, which would be detrimental to India.

Such were our concerns as I, along with Subedar Major Murmu, strolled along the coastline, inside the Battalion Headquarters, which was located near a Tamil village, north of Trincomalee. The Subedar Major was the senior-most JCO, who represented everyone in the battalion below the officer's rank. Subedar Major John Murmu was to retire after thirty years of service, the next year. A good, sincere, battle-hardened soldier, who according to age was the eldest person in the unit. He was wounded seriously in the 1971 war and survived after a major surgery. A God-fearing man who never hesitated to speak his mind, he spoke out on behalf of his troops whenever it was required and always rendered mature advice and caution to the Commanding Officer and the other officers. While always upholding the *izzat* and the reputation of the regiment, he not only ensured the welfare of the troops, but was also strict with training.

'Training Karo, Zinda Raho' (train to remain alive) was his oft-repeated motto. His eldest son was a Gentleman Cadet at the IMA and his second son was an Agricultural Extension Officer in Bihar.

His daughter had done an MSc in Mathematics and was married to an Army Officer from the Army Education Corps. His service of thirty years to the battalion and to his country was certainly a very distinguished one. I ensured that he would be granted the Honorary Rank of Captain on retirement. Subedar Major John Murmu had definitely lived a very honourable life. *'Sahib maine apni zindagi acchi tarah jee, Christ ki dua se'*, he said (Sahib, my life was well lived, by the grace of Christ). Seeing him and others like him, one could understand why the British were so fond of the Indian Army and considered them the most loyal and brave soldiers during World War I and II.

John Murmu and I strolled along the coastline. The sea was calm, serene and was a beautiful shade of blue. Numerous machine gun bunkers faced the sea. This was in order to protect the Battalion Headquarters. The LTTE had a deadly Naval Commando Force. Whenever they would see an opportunity, they would launch a raid at night or early in the morning, in fast-moving boats. Initially they would move their boats very slowly, while posing as local fishermen. Sensing any lack of alertness, they would converge with speed, cause heavy casualties and get away. And we did not even have Tamil-speaking soldiers with us.

John Murmu said thoughtfully, *'Sahib, yeh ajeeb paristhiti hai. Sri Lanka ke log Gautam Buddha ki pooja karte hain. Gautam Buddhaji ne toh Bihar, Bharat mein hi tapasya kia tha. Ham bhi Bihar Regiment ke hi hain. Toh yeh log bhi hamare jaise huen. Tamil log bhi Bharat se hi yahan aaye the. Ham Tamil logon ke khilaf jung kar rahe hain. Buddhist aur Hindu Tamil log yahan rahte hain sadiyon se. Yeh sab jo bhi ho raha hai, woh sahi nahi hai. Yeh galat hai.* (Sir, we are embroiled in a strange situation. The majority community of Sri Lanka worship Lord Buddha. Lord Buddha did his penance in Bihar, India. We are from the Bihar Regiment. So they are quite like us. The Tamils of this country also came here from India centuries ago. They have lived together here for eons. Why do they hate each other so deeply? Today we are fighting the Hindu Tamils. Whatever is happening here is wrong. This is just not fair.)'

'You are right John. I too wonder about these things. I realise that the troops are confused. I hope our Army never lands in such a thankless and confused situation ever again.'

'Soldiers need a very strong and understandable cause, to fight and die for. But I suppose the Army may have to fight for a cause which is best known by the rulers of the country. We are here to prevent the breakup of Sri Lanka. Such a situation will not be in the interests of India. It has many long-term implications. This is what I try to explain to the troops.'

'Sahib Jawan log itna samaj gaye hain. Lekin unke, hamare aur apke man mein kai aur sawaal hain, jinka uchit jawab kahin nahi hai. Agar India nahin chahta tha ki yeh mulk bikhar jaaye, to shuru se hi is halaat ko doosre tarike se sambhalna tha. Fauj ko itna ummeed rakhne ka haq hai ki desh ke neta aur Dilli ke adhikaari achche soojh-boojh ke saath nirnay le. Lekin itna ham aapko aashwasan dete hain ki ham log Regiment ki izzat, desh ki zarurat aur apni shaan aur garv ko barkarar rakhne ke liye larenge aur aapko let down *nahin karenge.'* Subedar Major John Murmu assured me, 'Sir, the troops have understood this much. But all of us have many more questions regarding this situation here, for which enough answers do not exist. If India wanted to prevent the breakup of this country, then our rulers should have handled this situation differently from the beginning. We military people have the right to expect that our rulers and authorities take such decisions very wisely. But I, on behalf of the troops, assure you that we will fight for the name of the Regiment, the expectations of our nation and our own pride and reputation. We shall not let you down.'

I appreciated the maturity, loyalty and devotion of my Subedar Major and patted him on his shoulders. I laughed aloud, telling him so. Finally, knowing that John Murmu had an uncanny sense of humour, I asked him to sum up the situation in a simple manner.

'Sahib, Dilli se Sri Lanka tak chamal ho raha hai', laughed John Murmu. (From Delhi to Sri Lanka chamal is happening.)

'Chamal kya hai? What is *chamal*?' I asked.

'*Ch…a* making at all levels. (F…ing each other at all levels)', laughed the Subedar Major and soon-to-be Honorary Captain John Murmu.

Swamy was a teacher in the school at the village of Kucchavelli, opposite which, near the sea shore, the Battalion Headquarters was located. Kucchavelli was a large fishing village south of Trincomalee city and port. It was a Tamil-dominated village. As part of IPKF, it was indeed a great challenge to touch the hearts and minds of the villagers for whom Prabhakaran was like Subhash Chandra Bose and LTTE akin to Azad Hind Fauj, in fact, much stronger and better organised.

Swamy was around sixty years old. He would often meet me in my Headquarters to discuss problems faced by the villagers. Extensive fishing, before the conflict, had made Kucchavelli very prosperous. Now various restrictions were imposed by the Sri Lankan government on fishing by Tamils. The LTTE had organised a commando-type, fast-attack naval force. These boats actively operated and even took on Sri Lankan Naval boats and ships in swift, surprising, devastating suicidal attacks. They also used local fishing boats for such operations.

My battalion rendered help in terms of medical care, running a kitchen to provide free meals to the poorest of the villagers, repairs of temples, schools etc damaged by Sri Lanka forces during operations prior to the arrival of the IPKF. We had provided sets of cricket gear to the villages around. We encouraged them to form one team each and organise inter-village matches. This became very popular. Expenditure for prize distribution was met by the unit. We were accepted by locals to some extent. After years of tragedy, some children were seen laughing and playing.

I could befriend Swamy easily. Swamy invited me, my Subedar Major and the unit panditji to his house for lunch on a Sunday. Since his house was adjacent to our army post, it was secure to go there. Still, some sentries were posted around the house by my Adjutant, Captain Sidhu.

Swamy's house was small, but very clean. We were welcomed by his wife and three daughters. There were small statues of Lord

Murugan in all corners of the room. A Tamil calendar, with the photo of the deity, hung on the wall facing the door. The room was simple, Spartan. There were four cane chairs and a seat was made over a big black steel trunk, which was neatly covered by thick cushion. Over the cushion, a red coloured cloth was spread as cover.

The eldest daughter, accompanied by another girl, served glasses full of coconut water to all of us. Off and on, as we drank up the delicious coconut water, a jug of more would arrive to replenish our glasses. I could sense that Swamy was keen to begin a conversation. He took off.

'Sir, I want to pour my heart out to you. Your office inside the Army Post was not the correct place to do so and more so, I wanted to study you and your men for a while first.'

'Please feel free to say whatever you want to Swamy. We too need to understand you better', I said encouragingly.

'Colonel, please tell me, are you motivated to come here, confronting the LTTE? You were expected to sympathise with them, as well as help them, as India was doing sometime back. Isn't this betrayal?'

'Well, there was a point in time during this conflict initially when it was necessary to help, because probably India felt that your cause was genuine. You all wanted to be granted more political space, autonomy and economic betterment which were being denied to you. We expected the government of Sri Lanka to realise their responsibilities towards their Tamil population and region.

'I must concede that India was slow to comprehend the deterioration of the situation here in Sri Lanka. May be, considerable mistakes in assessing the situation here were committed by the Indian government. Do remember, India itself experienced such challenges in Kashmir and the North East and understood that these problem take a long time to resolve.'

Swamy retaliated, 'But it did not take any time for India to decide to send the IPKF here to fight Tamils Sir.'

'Mr Swamy, I can assure you that we were not sent here with the mandate of fighting the LTTE. If that was so, our induction would not have been so hurried, in such unprepared conditions, without any knowledge of the terrain and battle condition. We came here as part of a larger autonomy process wherein, LTTE would gradually surrender their weapons against the guarantee that IPKF will ensure peace and security of Tamils. That is why we are called the Indian Peace Keeping Force.'

'Then, what happened, Sir?' queried Swamy, looking at me with great intensity.

'Suddenly the bar was raised by the LTTE towards achievement of their Eelam. India could never support break-up of Sri Lanka. Just forty years back, we faced the consequences of partition of India. It was a horrific experience.'

'As well as a necessary one, wasn't it?'

'Well, we could not have been assisters in the break up of Sri Lanka. The rest of the world would not have allowed it anyway. Instead of the IPKF, United Nation forces including troops from Pakistan, Bangladesh, China and other countries would have been here. You must see the broader picture. India could not have invaded Sri Lanka.'

Swamy smiled, 'So, India thought of invading the Tamil-dominated region of Sri Lanka. Very interesting. That proves that our ancient beliefs about ourselves were so true, which we were told about in our childhood.'

'Please tell me about this Swamy. I want to hear this. We need to reach out to what is in your heart deep down.'

'Perhaps, India did not think deep enough. But why shouldn't India have thought deep enough for Tamils? India thinks deep enough on Kashmir. It thinks deep enough on matters to do with the Indus Valley regions, Gangetic and Narbada Valley regions. Why does it think differently as one goes down South?'

'Come on, Swamy. This is not an objective statement. Kindly explain.'

'Okay, now let me explain, Sir. Please remember that Tamil culture is rooted in the ways of life in India, Sri Lanka, Malaysia, Singapore and across the globe.'

'True', I replied attentively.

'As you look around this room sir, you see Lord Murugan in all direction. He is the supreme deity, our Tamil God. Legend says that Lord Muruga, as a young boy, had an altercation with his brother Ganesha over a fruit. When his father Lord Shiva supported Ganesha, Muruga left Kailash to find his own group of people, the Tamils, and make Tamil Nadu his residence. So we are an aggrieved lot from those times', argued Swamy.

'But, Swamy. We should not rely so much on mythological stories and create difference between us', I reasoned. 'I do not view Shiva as a human being, but as a cosmic representation of divine power.'

'But then Sir, for most people in India and here, mythological stories are taken as real, just as Biblical events and other stories of that period in the Middle East are taken as real in other religions', retorted Swamy.

Swamy continued with passion. 'Sir, the problem is that many in India view Hindustan through the Indo-Aryan lense, which is a limited understanding of our vast religion or way of life. Have you heard of the term Kumari Kandam?'

'No, please tell me about it', I said.

'The term Kumari Kandam refers to an ancient continent with an ancient Tamil civilisation located, ironically, south of India, in the Indian Ocean. Its alternative names are Kumari Kandum and Kumari Nadu. According to modern science, of course, this continent is a pseudo-scientific concept.

'Ardent Tamils claim Kumari Kandam as the cradle of civilisation, which was lost to the sea in an oceanic catastrophe. The scientific theory of the continental shelf nullifies this belief. Some Hindu thinkers consider this term as a derivative of the Sanskrit words "Kumarika Khanda". However, Tamil revivalists do not accept this and consider this terms as purely a Tamil one, when Sanskrit did not exist. Some Tamils claim that this land was ruled by female rulers. There is some link with India's Kanya Kumari too.'

'This is interesting indeed', I chipped in. I was now being exposed to a different understanding of Tamil culture and perspectives.

Swamy was in full steam. I noticed that at this point, two elderly ladies were spreading mats on the clean floor of the verandah inside the house. Banana leaves were being laid in front of each mat. Lunch was being laid out in a meticulously organised manner.

'It is believed that Kanya Kumari of India was part of the original Kumari Kandam. Even present-day India, south of the Vindhyachal, was part of Kumari Kandam, also known as Lemuria', said Swamy confidently.

I was amused and also taken quite by surprise, hearing this version. A further statement by Swamy surprised me more. He said, 'Kumari Kandam was a society insulated from external influences and corruption, a place free of upper-caste Brahmins. These Brahmins were identified as descendants of Indo-Aryans during the Dravidian movement. This civilisation existed around 50,000 BCE which was eventually lost to sea around 16,000 BCE.'

'Today, all practices of the 20th century Tamil Hindu Society, such as superstitions and caste-based domination are actually corrupted practices under Indo-Aryan influences.'

'Is it true? Are such belief verified enough?' I asked.

'We Tamils here believe it to be true. We feel that Sanskrit deliberately kept the knowledge of Tamil greatness hidden from the public. Similarly, they chased Buddhism away to ensure that it does not dominate in India. After colonisation of the island nation, the British projected themselves as more civilised than the Tamils. Later, when the Sinhala population tried to subdue and oppress Sri Lankan Tamils in multiple ways, constantly humiliating them, this belief about Kumari Kandam, about Tamil superiority got a major boost.'

'But explain this to me Swamy. Don't you feel that such perceptions about a mythological past, without scientific and historical veracity, need to be changed in this modern age?' I insisted.

'But the answer is simple, Colonel Sir. Why should only we Tamils be expected to do so? Do the world of Christians, Muslims, Buddhists, Indo-Aryans reject their ancient past?'

'The first language spoken by humans was Tamil. All humans are descendants of ancient Tamils from Kumari Kandam. Do you know,

Sir, that all these aspects were taught in schools and colleges to Tamils in India and Sri Lanka up to the 20th century?'

I realised that lunch was about to be announced and so concluded, 'Swamy, we had a very interesting discussion with you. I will remember this interaction. While I do not know when and how this conflict will end, I am apprehensive about you all. We wish you well but we worry for you all here.'

Finally as my command tenure was coming to an end….

Grave mistakes were made in handling the Tamil issue in Sri Lanka.

At the end of my command tenure in Sri Lanka, I came to the conclusion that the IPKF operations in Sri Lanka were a pseudoevent, a contrived miscalculation at the national level. During such pseudoevents, the saga of bravery and sacrifices of those who died there or got severely wounded on foreign soil in a thankless mission usually get obscured.

It was a dishonest military intervention, devoid of a well thought-through and viable doctrine. It was devoid of awareness of the environmental ground realities and was without any coherent strategy. The nation failed once again to admire the Indian soldiers and junior officers for their courage and unflinching willingness to do whatever was demanded of them. These were acts of faith for which they were being utilised, thinking that they were addressing genuine and serious national security challenges which required competent men of intellectual integrity and character at the highest levels.

Our Generals should have insisted that they were given objectives that were clear, consistent and were backed by adequate resources and which were achievable within a reasonable time frame. Military hierarchy should not have gone overboard by assuring the ministers that they have done whatever was asked of them. They should not have shown a servile desire to display a 'CAN DO' spirit. They certainly should not have acquiesced to dubious propositions which were made by the civilian MoD bosses. A similar situation existed in 1984, when the Golden Temple was stormed by the Army.

A floundering South Asian giant, more due to its geographical size and population, with no culture of strategic vision, should first try to build up capacities to become a medium-sized power, before dreaming of becoming a major power.

Accordingly, it should decide what kind of military it needs and is prepared to pay for. One needs to learn to walk properly before trying to run and fall down badly. Unfortunately, unlike the American, the British military, the Pakistan Army and even the Bangladesh Army, Generals in Indian Army are not encouraged to express their different viewpoints freely. The citizens of the nation do not get to know about their viewpoints.

The IPKF operation was doomed for a stalemate due to political obduracy, lethally combined with bullish optimism of the Generals. No serious attempt appears to have been made to understand the capabilities and steely resolve of the LTTE, the local support they commanded. The Indian nation moved on in such a lackadaisical scenario, but the military institution got crowned with the stigma of a botched operation. Such are the games the rulers of the nation play at times. Not having strategic vision is bad enough, but pretences of strategic vision is very dangerous.

My teenage daughter, studying in a boarding school at Calcutta at the time, wrote a small poem on her Dad's going to Sri Lanka:

Dad's gone far away,
Far from all of us,
Amidst the fire, commotion, death and blood,
Where today so many eyes are in flood.
About himself, he is careless,
And of the dreadful place, fearless,
Where all hopes, dreams and attempts are futile,
When a sudden attack takes place for a while.
We must be strong and not show weakness,
But part with him with a smile of sweetness,

He goes to bring peace and love among men,
And bring sunshine to the dark den.

This young girl wrote this neither as an Indian, Sri Lankan or Tamil but just as a daughter whose father was a part of this tragic conflict. She only expressed her child-like feelings. There must have been many children whose fathers were part of this war, having similar feelings.

As the operations in Sri Lanka came to and an end, within a few years in Kashmir, terrorism erupted. After years of careful planning, the Pakistan Army unleashed a new form of war on India. An undeclared, yet viciously conducted asymmetrical, ruthless war of terrorism. The battalion in which I was commissioned, and in which I participated during the 1971 war, was fully embroiled in this new kind of war, called counter-terrorism.

The battalion was now led by Lt Colonel Gaur. Gaur was a daredevil Commanding Officer. He led by personal example, always in front during dangerous situations. The troops adored him. The unit regained control in their vast area of responsibility, inflicting heavy casualties on the well-trained, equipped terrorists from Pakistan. The unit too suffered casualties.

In one major encounter with a very tough group of terrorists, the fighting was intense and long drawn. This group was determined to fight to death while trying to inflict maximum damage to the Army. Lt Col Gaur was one of the best Commanding Officers to match this situation. He led the troops fearlessly. He realised that the situation was too serious.

The fiercest encounter during this period ended in the death of all the terrorists. Lt Col Gaur, the gallant Commanding Officer, too sacrificed his life in the process. Lt Col Gaur was posthumously awarded the Ashok Chakra, the highest national award for gallantry. The tradition of this battalion for gallantry, exemplified in the 1971 war, continued in the true spirit of the Indian Armed Forces. That was of a life lived with honour, gallantry and patriotism. India is blessed with a great professional and patriotic military.

SCHOLAR SOLDIER

National Defence College

State which separates its scholars from its warriors will have its thinking done by cowards and fighting done by fools.

—Thucydides

Twenty first century is the century of scholar soldiers. Warriors not only brave, but well read and high-tech, who can foresee changes in the nature of war and evolve into future military thinkers.

It was a sabbatical year for me. I was a student once again, at the National Defence College (NDC), a think-tank for comprehensive national security. This college was established on 27 April 1960. The aim laid down for the NDC was that 'The NDC would provide joint training and instructions to senior (military) service and civil service officers. The study would relate to the strategic, economic, political and the industrial aspects of national security. Based on the above aims, the scope of study is planned to include an examination of internal and external threats to the security of India, as well as possible trends for the next ten years. Studies would include an analysis of diverse factors such as policies of other nations, conflicts over vital economic interests or territorial claims and factional, communal and political interferences. Members of the course would also analyse the formation of national strategy for various contingencies including the outbreak of war.'

The plan was to bring selected senior officers from various organs of the government and friendly foreign countries for forty-seven weeks of study. It was to foster better understanding, mutual cooperation and desirable linkages in the national, regional and international security-related fields with friendly foreign countries.

Now, as a Brigadier, I considered myself immensely lucky to have been nominated for this prestigious course in 1998. During the course, India conducted its nuclear tests at Pokharan amidst great international furore and scepticism. Pakistan followed suit, soon thereafter. The study on national security assumed serious proportions during this course.

Among the most debated issues was the scope for military confrontation between two nuclear armed nations who shared a long international border and an active line of control dividing the disputed parts of Kashmir. Most of the civil services officers and the foreign members at the course ruled out the existence of such a window for a conventional conflict. In fact, some of them advocated reduction in military spending and in the size of the Armed Forces, since India had no interest in initiating a conventional war with any country.

Indian nationhood, since independence, had always nurtured a negative attitude towards its military, particularly at the level of politics and bureaucracy. The military officers of India felt otherwise. The MoD officials started fantasising again about India becoming a superpower. China was promptly declared as India's number one enemy, when even the USA had refrained from declaring it so. Instead of acknowledging the fact that India should have taken this bold step to become a nuclear power two decades earlier, when Pakistan had not been in a position to respond, the country celebrated. It was like India and Pakistan were simultaneously celebrating Diwali together.

One witty Brigadier, doing the course at the NDC, described this jubilation aptly as, 'one of the most spectacular premature ejaculation of exuberance by ignorant fools'. How else could one have described the celebration of a capability which should have been acquired by the late 1970s? Yes, of course, things would have been difficult then. Powerful nations would have imposed restrictions on India, and anyway, many nations did. The price might have been heavy. And it was, despite the fact that India had no bomb until 1998, only a peaceful detonation in Indira Gandhi's time.

A nation, which was clear about its strategic interests, especially amidst the fact that some of the P5 nations who were responsible for ensuring that nuclear weapons technology did not spread were helping Pakistan and North Korea, had no other choice. India had a case.

At times, a nation had to endure challenges in order to recover its dignity. Even North Korea had the guts to be nearly at par with India on this issue. It was as if Pakistan wanted to dare India and see how far we would go. Would we use the nuclear weapon or not? As if to test India, the Kargil War, supposedly a conventional war between two nuclear-armed neighbours, took place in 1999. The same people, who had valiantly declared China as the number one enemy, were frantically running around now like headless chickens.

With a similar mindset, India had majestically declared in 1959 that any attack on Nepal and Bhutan would be taken as an attack on India. In 1962, when China attacked India, its leaders had no wherewithal to respond with. Half of the number of Indian military officers who did this course were soon to be actively involved as part of the Northern Command and Army Headquarters in a very arduous, complex, and bloody conflict in the Kargil sector.

At the NDC, all course members were sub-divided into various Integrated Analysis Groups (IAGs). Each IAG comprised about fifteen officers. It was a balanced mix of civil services officers, foreign military officers and Indian military officers. A Major General from the Army or an equivalent-level officer from Air Force or Navy and a Joint Secretary-level officer from the Indian Administrative Service (IAS) or Indian Foreign Service (IFS) were allotted to each IAG as Senior Directing Staff of the faculty.

During one study relating to the Indian economy, its governance, the practice of democracy and its effects on national security, one IAG room was throbbing with high octane discussion. The IAG had a five-week time to produce a joint paper and was required to give a power point presentation. The presentation would culminate with a grilling question and answer session, with the rest of the course members.

Brigadier Mehta, the nominated IAG leader, opened the discussion.

'Friends, despite a good GDP growth, India is the only South Asian power which is quite below its potential. Economic growth has mainly benefitted about twenty five per cent of the population. The system of governance has created high inflation, rampant corruption, unemployment and underemployment. About 500 million people are excluded and are not stakeholders of this growth and in the nation-building process. Before we can start discussing good governance in India, we need to be honest to admit the cesspool of abject poverty in India. How can we have comprehensive national security under such stark circumstances? Let us discuss this first.'

One IAS officer, Raghavender, did not like this one bit. He said testily, 'I think it has become fashionable for Indians to deride their government. India has made stupendous progress over the last sixty years. It is a thriving democracy. Every five years, people get the chance to change the government at the Centre. I have the details of the progress made in agriculture, industry, science and technology which we can share on such issues. Poverty levels have gone down and massive schemes have been launched at a scale that has been globally recognised. Rural people have access to the Public Distribution System. Massive investments in rural development, education and health have been done. During our presentation, we must highlight all such positive achievements.'

Brig Mehta replied, 'Yes of course Raghu. You take on this part of highlighting the positives. However, please also be receptive to contrary viewpoints, as we carry on with our study. We shall get varied inputs as excellent economists and analysts of national and international levels will be talking to us in the coming weeks. The fact is that after fifty years of independence, we are yet quite low in the Asian pecking order and are still struggling to emerge out of the South Asian environment. South Asia is perhaps the most laggard region of Asia in any case. Under present conditions, India is getting increasingly vulnerable in terms of national security.'

Brig John Atkins (of the US Army) intervened to say, 'We have been on two tours so far, to Madhya Pradesh and Andhra Pradesh, where we have observed the ground realities. Gentlemen, I can give the perspective from the developed Western world. If you choose to highlight twenty positives to prove that India is on its way to become a global power, it would be true. If you choose to highlight twenty negatives to prove that India is lagging far behind even in Asia, that too will sound very convincing. As foreigners, we see both aspects in ample order. Though I admit the negatives are very serious ones and it is easier to be pessimistic. We do see a tremendous amount of potential energy in India. Kinetic (realised) energy does not do justice to the potential energy. India's internal security under its Home Ministry, both at the Centre and at the States, seems very vulnerable indeed. India's police force is neither trained nor equipped and nor amply led to take on the internal security challenges. And may I caution you not to underestimate the Naxals.'

'As many as 220 out of about 626 districts are under Naxal control effectively. Such a massive uprising would surely have international linkages', Atkins quipped.

'In order to realise one's true potential, one has to first be honest about locating and accepting the actual bottom line. Then only can one rise to the next level. It is up to you all to do so without taking counsel of your fears and egos, or choosing to be in the denial mode. The fact is that Asia and the world will be better off, if India achieves its true potential', concluded Atkins.

Brig Mehta smiled. 'The spirit of NDC lies in listening patiently to others who come from diverse fields having responsible jobs, with an open mind to learn, imbibe, in order to broaden one's perspectives and correct one's mindsets. Your perceptions are very valuable inputs for us all. By the time we complete this one year long course, we all will be more evolved, balanced and knowledgeable. Thank you, Atkins.'

Brig Sukhwinder from the Artillery chipped in, 'There are hundred million people in India who have no electricity. A similar number do have electricity connections, but get only a couple of hours of electricity supply each day. Our human development indices are pathetic by Asian and even African standards. We all know that maximum infants who die due to malnutrition in the world, are from India. We seem to have reconciled ourselves to the fact that we can never match China in manufacturing. China has done better than India in curbing corruption. How can our politicians and bureaucrats feel so smug and satisfied with India's performance? They only display gross apathy to over 500 million chronically-poor Indians. Atkins was correct to suggest that we must honestly accept our bottom line and then improve things, rather than rationalising our failures and overstressing our rather limited successes by quoting official statistics and data.'

Another IAS officer, Mittal, quipped rather agitatedly, 'I don't feel we need to be so pessimistic about ourselves. We need to fully appreciate and understand the complexities of governing India, which is a veritable salad bowl of all religions of the world and of various castes and ethnicities. Look at the sheer number of humanity here and their diversity. On top of that, a flood of expectations and hopes were unleashed by the government since 1991. Look at the large railway system which has to be run. Look at the vast historical exploitation of India, done repeatedly by invaders who ruled over it, for over centuries. Just compare where we were in 1947, and where we are now. Imagine the large international borders we have, ranging from deserts, marshlands, high-density forests to the high-altitude Himalayas. We have a long coastline. The issue of governance is of massive proportions and challenges. Governing India is a massive challenge. Please be fair in your analysis, friends.'

Group Captain Javed of the Indian Air Force, with his typical disarming smile, exclaimed, 'Yaar Mittal, you are right. No one can minimise the challenges facing India. Bureaucrats have a tough complex job. You all have to handle politicians of all types. The range of issues and challenges you all handle are just too complex. Some of us here have relatives in IAS and civil services. We all know their difficulties. While I lament the massive power and associated derivatives that they enjoy, I would never like to be in their place.'

'Yes, we have very long, the most difficult and awfully challenging borders and disputed territories to protect. The Indian military has no choice but to do it', continued Javed. 'The Indian military has to also protect North East India and Jammu Kashmir from secessionist tendencies. We are frequently called in, at times, at the drop of a hat by the District Collector, to help civil administration in numerous crises and situations. While doing all these duties, we do get exposed to the dire state of the delivery of governance. It makes some of us very sceptical and most of us rather cynical. Here, at the NDC, when we share our feelings as part of learning, please do not misunderstand us. We too have enormous problems in defending India. But if we overstate these difficulties to you all and give in, you too would not feel confident about our ability to do our duty, in order to protect the nation. An unprotected or unprotectable nation is not a nation at all. Similar is the case of good governance. Non-delivery of good governance is perhaps the most unpatriotic and damaging act.

'Eventually, the issue is not about India emerging as a super power. We are very very far from it and we all know it, even if it is fashionable to discuss being a superpower to soothen Indian egos. Self-delusion is a common human fault line. The issue is about the delivery of good governance. If eighty five paise per rupee gets siphoned off, how can governance be delivered in a subcontinental nation like India? I think this is the real bottom line which never gets addressed seriously, for seemingly obvious reasons. The frustrations and lack of hope for nearly five hundred million Indians is a serious internal security concern.'

Brigadier Griffith (from Australia), an extremely popular, jovial course member had been quietly sipping coke and smiling during the discussion so far. He joined in, 'I have spent a few months here in India. I am both fascinated and upbeat about this amazing country, despite the truly stark poverty and pathetic conditions in rural and urban areas. I didn't have to look deeper to see the true India. Everything is visible and open.'

'I am amazed at the grim determination, steely resolve and the tolerance of Indians in rural areas. Grassroots level Indians face life with such character, poise and equanimity. I sense equilibrium and enlightenment here. Despite all the trials and tribulations of a bare existence, as well as the pathetic conditions, they believe in lakhs of gods. In the developed West, with all its affluence, many people are finding it silly to believe in religion seriously. I personally feel a sense of unconditional optimism here. India will overcome its problems. It needs more time and possibly more help. For the sake of a better Asia and a stable world, India must rise. The only thing I would like to shout and say is that for heavens sake, move your bloody arses together and faster, instead of buggering each other. Now can we have some beer?'

The entire IAG laughed aloud. Brig Mehta declared a beer break and announced an afternoon session for further discussions.

The National Defence College is indeed a significant nation-building institution. It brought senior bureaucrats of central government services and selected Brigadiers and equivalent-level military officers of the Indian Air Force and Navy, together. It was a sabbatical of one year of study, knowledge sharing and upgrading and broadening of visions as well as understanding each other and removing cobwebs of faulty perceptions about each other. Foreign officers brought in their own experiences and perceptions of how they felt about India and its national security paradigm as well as global issues. Lifelong bonds and camaraderie were fostered. An unique blend of professional and personal relations were forged, with sharing meals and bonhomie in each other's homes being a regular affair.

Indian military officers who attended the course were generally those who had seen thirty years of service. Civil services bureaucrats had sixteen to eighteen years of service, though of equivalent civilian rank. All the civil servants were assured of going beyond the rank of Joint Secretary, which was equivalent to Major General and beyond;

within a few years after the course. Army officers represented only about twenty per cent of their entire batch, who had risen to the rank of Brigadiers and were yet not assured of the rank of Major General and above. Eighty per cent of their batch mates would retire as Colonels due to lack of vacancies, despite having done well in numerous courses and challenging assignments, having received war decorations and wound medals as well as Presidential recognition for meritorious services. They retired at the age of fifty-six and were forced to seek employment in the corporate sector, though they did eventually distinguished themselves there.

The condition of those below the officer's ranks were worse. Jawans retired at the age of thirty-five to forty-years. They were the only Central government employees who retired so early. It is of national importance to keep the military young. Service conditions necessitated this.

When the military officers met their civil counterparts for a year, in a purely academic environment, it was like an interaction of two different cultures, even akin to different planets, initially. NDC converted them into colleagues and friends during the course. Gradually, each learned to appreciate the challenges and difficulties of the other side and realised the need to work together for the complex process of nation-building.

During a social gathering in the bar of the NDC, Ponappa (IAS), Swamy (IAS) and I were having a drink together and discussing such issues. Ponappa said, 'friend, just like all of you, when we passed out of the IAS Academy in Mussourie, we too were very motivated. We dreamt of changing the face of India. We started our first posting in a district of a State with lots of idealism. Soon the ground realities of politics in India dawned on us. It would be inappropriate for me to speak of all the details, but during this course, all of you learnt about some of these ground realities. Some of us did withstand the unjust, corrupt pressures and kept suffereing the inconveniences and humiliations of frequent transfers. Luckily, our Constitution protected us from greater damage. Some of us just couldn't take such pressures from elected representatives and their goons. So the transition towards compromise and acceptance of ground realities and the eventual absorption into the system took place gradually.'

Swamy chipped in, 'I would like to say this to all my military friends. We have seen your lifestyles, your family lives, your smart, articulate and well educated wives and the upbringing of your children. Your Regimental ethos, sense of belonging, organisational pride, lifelong linkages to your traditions and ethos are exceptional in comparison to Indian society's. You may envy the power we enjoy, our career progression and perhaps our personal wealth. You may lament the fact that all of us have an assured job till sixty years of age. In fact, most of us never really retire thereafter. You can demand that every gentleman cadet passing out of the military academy also get the assured rank of a Major General, which is equivalent of a Joint Secretary or be fully compensated in lieu. You could demand that the same be applied to your soldiers. You may have many more such grievances. But let me tell you, our lives are not easy. Every time a crude, uneducated and uncouth elected politician humiliates us, something in us dies. The superiors, under whom you all serve, are really superiors. They have much more character and leadership qualities. They groom you and they look after you. Our case is so different.'

Ponappa added with a smile, 'The quality of life which you live and the honour that you enjoy are far superior to ours. You do not have to feel aggrieved. Finally, you all also need to guard against corruption, which is slowly creeping into your system. You all know it well enough. Don't feel happy for the fact that within your system, the levels of corruption are very low. Yes it is so. The levels of corruption increase in direct ratio of the opportunities. Your problem is also "top down". In a decade or so, you will recall what I am telling you now. For the sake of the nation, I hope I am wrong in my assessment. But believe me, I am more aware of this than you are. You have not served in Delhi till you came to the NDC. You have served more in the operational areas and this is why you may be a bit unaware of the growing tendency of corruption in the military. Being better than us, which you will always be, is no consolation.'

'Thank you my friends', I exclaimed. 'You both have a point and I am not totally unaware of such growing tendencies in the Armed Forces. Some of us, during this course, tend to go overboard in criticising the bureaucrats. Many guest speakers blamed the bureaucrats and the politicians during their talks on India's performance in various spheres, which also affected our existing mindsets. I do hope that excellent officers like you become our future Defence Secretaries and senior bureaucrats at the MoD. It will do the country good. I do have a relative of mine in the IAS. I know for sure, he is an extremely honest and capable officer.'

'One last thing, that I wish to add', said Ponappa. 'After this course, you military officers will face cut-throat competitions in your promotions. Many of you will not go beyond the rank of Major General. However, most of you will retire with pride and elan and will still lead a fairly good retired life. Your children will be better groomed and be better human beings, unlike many other children whose parents have enjoyed immense power and wealth. Never feel that you have lost out very much in the larger aspects of life. Never lose out on your core strengths.'

Swamy added, 'Moreover, never blame our democracy for our ills. A nation that cannot handle the worst aspects of democracy does not deserve its best fruits. India is trying to manage its democracy. Governance in India is not really lying in the intensive-care units of Delhi, or State capitals. It is sick but it can regain its health. It will. The pressure of the people and civil society will make it work better. Our millennium kids will make good leaders, administrators, innovators, wealth creators, scientists, entrepreneurs, politicians and soldiers. They need to be handled and groomed differently. In a land of a billion plus, a million of our best of our younger generation of human resources can change India in a decade or two.'

I nodded in agreement with the views of these two excellent bureaucrats. I said, 'You both are right. Someone rightly said in one of the lectures, that India never misses an opportunity to miss an opportunity. If we miss out on reaping a demographic dividend and land up in a situation of a youth bulge sliding helplessly into the quagmire of the bottom of the population pyramid, then we have had it. India's strategic pirouette must focus on avoiding such a situation. The younger generation must be partners of India's growth, more so than its politicians and bureaucrats. They will assert our nationhood soon.'

'Similar is the situation in the Indian military today. The junior officers must be allowed to express their views more freely. The military hierarchy and bureaucracy must be more sensitive in handling our millennium generation of young soldiers and junior officers. I am not sure if this has even begun to happen. Stiff-collared and grim senior officers who live in ivory towers of cantonments too need to introspect. Young Jawans and junior officers are highly aware of everything about the organisation.'

I further added with a naughty smile, 'you all should be aware of the feelings of the young officers in the Army. They usually joke during social events that Indian military faces two strong adversaries. They are the ISI of Pakistan and the IAS of India, in that close order. The former is ever scheming to inflict a thousand cuts on the Indian military and the latter is always busy keeping us stunted by cutting us down to size always.'

Swamy responded before Ponappa could. 'While the first part about the ISI is true, the second impression is not so. However, the point is noted. Such perceptions should not be ignored. We too need to introspect. Friend, but for this wonderful one-year interaction at the National Defence College, we would never have discussed these issues so frankly anywhere.'

Ironically, the Kargil War that took place after our NDC course was not a typical conventional war. Two nuclear-capable nations could not have declared a conventional war and fought it.

It was actually a typical set of tactical battles which were part of an asymmetrical warfare. It was a value-addition to the use of terrorism as a method of waging a persistent, bloody, yet undeclared war against India in Kashmir.

As insurgency in Kashmir valley got upgraded to sponsored terrorism, it was a paradigm shift in the nature of warfare, which could be fought in spite of the backdrop of a strategic (not real) nuclear war which had engulfed India and Pakistan. In response to such sponsored terrorism, as a new form of warfare, no country could respond with nuclear weapons. India's nuclear capability stood effectively emasculated.

The occupation by the Pakistan Army, masquerading as militants, of scores of unoccupied mountain tops could have been a serious threat to Siachen as well as India's ability to maintain its forces in the distant regions of Kashmir and Ladakh.

This situation could not be redeemed by Generals, national think-tanks and the egoistic security experts of the nation. This dangerous and daring provocation by Pakistan could only be redeemed by the brave soldiers, junior officers and the best Commanding Officers of India's Infantry battalions as well as Artillery regiments and daring Air Force pilots, in the occupied territories, in hand-to-hand battles.

Kargil was a brilliant tactical plan by Pakistan, although a strategic blunder. It shamed India and its newly-acquired nuclear weapons-power status. Many brave hearts amongst the best of the Indian military had to die to win back the occupied peaks and restore the situation to normalcy.

It was insurgency, which escalated into terrorism and peaked into a daring asymmetrical warfare of a different kind. The nature of warfare was evolving and changing. A militarily weaker nation could challenge a stronger nation, look at it squarely eye-to-eye and dare it, notwithstanding the threat of nuclear weapons. India was busy using its best and very-limited imported weaponry and Air Force capabilities, not on Pakistan, but on its own soil, on high mountain tops, each occupied by not more than a dozen well-armed soldiers. India was truly shaken and nicely screwed for a while.

JAMMU & KASHMIR

War and Peace in Paradise

In historical events great men—so called—are but the labels that serve to give a mane to an event, and like labels, they have the last possible connection with the event itself. Every action of theirs, that seems to them an act of their own free will, is in an historical sense not free at all but in bondage to the whole course of previous history, and predestined from all eternity.

—Lev Tolstoy

Military conflict between two nuclear powers in the most impoverished and peripheral region of Asia, called South Asia, is something not to be taken casually.

It is at such times that one consciously wonders about resolution of the Jammu and Kashmir imbroglio, including that of Pakistan occupied Kashmir (PoK). Will it be a victory for India or Pakistan? No. It will be a prize with a price. A prize won by South Asia in particular, Asia in general. The price for this prize has to be paid by India and Pakistan. This payment will eventually prove to be a wise investment for the future prosperity of the people of both, India and Pakistan.

My posting as the Commander of the brigade at Tangdhar, also known as the Tithwal sector of Kashmir, was a hard transition from the theoretical world of NDC to the real, live, conflict-ridden region of South Asia. The Tangdhar position was a bulge emanating westerwards, from the Pir Panjal mountain range towards Muzzafarabad, in Pakistan occupied Kashmir. This sensitive sector is surrounded by Pakistani posts on three sides and remains totally cut off from Kashmir valley for five months every winter. To maintain the brigade and the local population, winter stocking takes place, which is an elaborate logistical exercise annually. Weather rarely permits even helicopters from coming in during this period. In those days, due to its geographic isolation during winters, a small military hospital was built nearby.

The Kargil operations started soon enough after I took up posting here. The entire Line of Control became hot and active. Heavy artillery shelling from both sides became a regular feature. As the Pakistani Army started interdicting the Srinagar–Leh Road in the Kargil Sector, the entire Line of Control got activated and a free-for-all shelling erupted. Casualties, including those of civilians, resulted consequently. Many innovations, improvisations and tactical plans for artillery shelling as well as for rocket and missile firings were resorted to by both the sides.

Being surrounded by Pakistani posts from the three sides, the Tangdhar post had to be three times more proactive in its response. Farthest-flung posts, which were in eyeball-to-eyeball contact with the Pakistani side, had to be alert day and night and had to be ready for sudden attacks. Any mistake or careless move attracted instant sniper fire and resulted in casualties. An offensive spirit was the only option. The brave hearts in these posts only slept in turns during day time. All had to keep awake during the night.

Soldiers and junior officers of both the armies were tough and fiercely patriotic. Display of raw bravery and courage by both the sides were beyond the imagination of civil societies as well as national security theorists of both the countries.

I often wondered whether the government of India and its people will ever fully realise what a fine military they had. If they did, then the Armed Forces would have been much better nurtured, equipped and would have been provided with superior border infrastructure than Pakistan, which was a much smaller neighbour. Not only the Indian government, the Indian Army too had become complacent about its Infantry and Artillery. It was also a case of the failure of the Army's leadership to thump the table very loudly in the corridors of North and South Block, demanding adequate intelligence and equipment, accompanied by superior strategy.

In this case, it was the Infantry and Artillery arms of the Indian Army which had to bear the brunt of the fighting in high altitude, in the massive mountain ranges of Kashmir. It was a meaningless conflict, initiated by the Pakistani Army who were the real rulers of their country. Its civilian government was just an appendix, a mask masquerading as a democracy. How could the military of a self-proclaimed democracy be so disdainful of its politicians and the people? For the Pakistani Army, their stranglehold of religion was more important than their nation. For the Indian Armed Forces, the nation itself was God. An important and critical difference between the two militaries, I thought.

During this period, the Indian Army was displaying a tendency of overstressing the importance of major, large-scale, demonstrative peace-time military exercises in the deserts of Rajasthan and the plains of Punjab. Stress was on imagining armoured and mechanised columns breaking majestically into Pakistan, after the Infantry suffered massive casualties and captured initial objectives. It was like a corny fantasisation of the battles that were fought during the Second World War, sans live enemy opposition and the dynamics of the bitter battles.

During such exercises, some Army Generals even started displaying the swagger of Rommel, Montgomery and Manstein, all rolled into one. Such exercises, though necessary for limited purposes, were not so professionally honest in their conduct and the lessons that had to be learnt. India was soon to be taught a few more lessons by a neighbour, one-seventh its size.

As the Kargil conflict commenced, all the other brigades holding the Line of Control (LoC) were in a HOT WAR mode. Many options for offensive plans were examined while the intense firing, shelling and encounters were on. A real war looked imminent, with all options being open. The local villagers on both sides got engulfed in the conflict. Collateral damage was inevitable as numerous villages existed near the LoC. Villagers residing on both sides of LoC are very unfortunate during any Indo-Pak conflict. To the utter chagrin of the Indian Army, despite severe provocations, no credible conventional war options existed.

Pakistan, displaying astute tactical brilliance, had managed to conduct a limited conflict, forcing India to fight its battles within its own remotest and toughest terrains in Kashmir. One of the largest military forces in the world was helpless in its options to enlarge the conflict, and even go for a limited victory across the Line of Control. This would have resulted in two nuclear-armed nations going for full-scale war.

Neither were the two countries equipped to do so, nor would the global powers allow such a thing to happen. The Indian Army had starved its Artillery of medium guns and the Infantry was not equipped for a full-scale war. Pakistan again exposed the reality of India not even being a regional power amidst its immediate neighbourhood. Of course, the anglicised, English-speaking, smart, astute, desk-borne security strategists never got discouraged. The top brass of the Indian military, in any case, played no real role in India, with their wings clipped by various means.

On the other hand, the Pakistani Army were the real rulers of Pakistan, behind the smoke screen of a controlled, pseudo-democracy. Lord Macaulay decried the Last Emperor of India as 'a mock sovereign immured in a gorgeous state prison'. Something akin to this was the state of democracy in Pakistan.

Over a period of time, the military top brass of Major Generals and above in India had developed a whatever-istic tendency. Whenever a war-like situation arose, they parroted to the government, that they would fight the war with whatever capabilities they possessed in terms of weaponry and military hardware and infrastructure.

During one such intense exchange of artillery, in the Tangdhar Sector, one young woman ventured out of the dug-in family bunker, to gather the cattle to a safe area. An artillery shell blew up one of her legs and shrapnel pierced her body. She was brought to the Military Hospital by some brave local men. She was treated in the underground surgical operation room since the hospital was also under shelling. Her leg had to be amputated but her life was saved. Next day, I visited the Military Hospital to look up the casualties, which included a few troops and some civilians. This lady was lying in bed. When I inquired about her welfare, she smiled and said weakly, 'Sir, Allah has saved my second leg and my life, to enable me to look after my children. Now I am under Allah's care forever. There is nothing now for me to worry about.' I was visibly moved by this brave and spiritual woman. I pondered that human beings of such great quality existed on both sides of the LoC, who so stoically bore the brunt of senseless conflicts between the two countries.

I decided that such people of Tangdhar deserve to be looked after, with all the resources at our disposal. I solemnly saluted her and exclaimed, '*Main app jais oonche darze ke insaan ko salute karta hoon. Allah aapko hamesha salaamat rakhe.*' (I salute a human being of such a high calibre. May Allah always protect you.) When such brave, spiritual, yet ordinary people interpreted their religion with such purity of purpose and drew strength and inspiration from it, they enhanced the credibility and respectability of religion. This was a lesson I registered as I departed from the hospital.

In the Tangdhar valley lived a very pious Sufi Muslim gentleman. He would walk around the villages and hamlets, singing verses praising Allah. He was very spiritual and always had a divine smile on his face. One day, as I was moving in a convoy, I saw him and had a small chat in his humble hut which was under an old walnut tree. I asked him for his brief on the genesis of the Kashmir problem. He replied sadly that Kashmiris historically were liberal in their interpretation of Islam. *Kashmiriat* was in their past and had been a way of life. It had always been a land of Pirs (people who expressed love for Allah along with Kashmiri characteristics of love for nature and its beauty).

He explained, 'Sahib, religious fundamentalism was anathema to the Kashmiri culture, though we were always good Muslims. Extreme interpretations of Islam have taken us away from nature and its beautiful manifestations. Nature is so divine. If you don't love nature, how can you love at all? How can religion be loveless with no music, poetry and singing in praise of the Allah? How can Allah be all merciful, all compassionate when human beings are not? One should wonder. Any pilgrimage to Allah has to pass through love for humanity, empathy and kindness to the down trodden, in all their diversity all around the world.' I was amazed.

The Pakistan Army detachments in the Kargil sector had occupied scores of high mountain tops, which the Indian Army had not occupied during winters. Now, those very areas had to be recaptured by the Indian Army infantry, supported by Artillery and Air Force at a heavy cost of lives and limbs.

It was now a bitter fight between the troops and the young officers of both the armies. The gallant junior officers, unit level Commanding Officers and the indomitable Indian Jawans went about recapturing these areas, while being highly disadvantaged due to the enemy being well entrenched on the commanding heights of the mountain tops.

While this was being done, the Kargil battle should have shaken up the military top brass, the MoD and the Government of India. Unfortunately, a nation which did not have to physically fight for a long duration and hard for its independence, took a long time to understand and value its military.

The nation would, in due course of time, fail to convert this bitter experience of Kargil into a major revaluation of the military structure and related capacity-building. Wrong people would take the credit for this victory and short-term political benefits would be reaped by the national leaders.

In future, the military top brass need to learn to thump the table more forcefully about serious gaps in military capabilities than hithertofore. This will ensure that military power must match national intentions always. Direct access to the Prime Minister once a month or so is a functional requirement in a nation which has grave security environment. Babudom cannot come in the way of this necessity. They are not directly responsible for the military dimensions of national security. They have enough secretarial responsibilities in this aspect. It does not serve any purpose by saying that 'we shall fight with whatever we have' during a conflict.

The Indian military will never be able to fathom why its elected leaders and bureaucracy have such an attitude towards the military. This is the Army which has been most comfortable with civilian supremacy and democracy in South Asia. They are as loyal to the Constitution as its makers were. This remains a strange paradox in India.

With the closure of the Kargil War, there was a relative respite from cross-border shelling. Infiltration of terrorists, with support of the Pakistani Army posts giving covering fire, continued unabated to become almost a ritualistic affair. Frequently, clashes and encounters took place. The infiltrating terrorists were extremely well-trained, motivated and well-equipped. A fair degree of local support in terms of guides, sanctuaries in some villages and dense jungles as well as intelligence on whereabouts of Indian Army counter-infiltration forces etc was available to them. The terrorists, when encountering the Indian Army, fought hard and displayed no intention to surrender. There were cases when on being grievously wounded, they would arm a grenade and blow themselves up, as Indian Army troops came to capture them, causing more casualties.

On mere suspicion about any Kashmiri being an informer for Indian forces, they would slit the throat of the person in front of the entire family. Then they would clean their bloodied hands by forcing the wife or mother of the victim to pour water on their hands. Such stark cruelty would send a message to every village around, not to inform the Indian security forces about infiltrator activities and movements. These incidents were carried out quite frequently in areas which were far away from the security posts. Any brave police officer's family would be ruthlessly punished. I wondered if the people in Delhi were aware of such stark ground realities under which the security forces were functioning in Kashmir. Even people in Srinagar were far away from the ground realities of the condition of the villagers who were living in remote hills and valleys near the LoC. After all, politicking always had been the most critical activity while governing India. People and lives never had much value.

One day, the local village head, Mujib, an ex MLA, invited me for a meal and an interaction with some village elders of Tangdhar, in his house. Since the host was a prominent land lord of the area, his was a big house. The menu was sumptuous and the quantity of chicken, lamb, vegetables and rotis provided were enough to feed at least twenty more people. The aroma of ghee, saffron and herbs dominated the huge hall in which we were seated. In a long welcome speech mixed with political overtones, the host talked about how the people of Tangdhar valley along with the Army, had experienced the intense shelling during the conflict and how the Army had treated civilian casualties in their Military Hospital. He also appreciated the fact that thirty young students had been taken on a trip to Delhi, Agra, Lucknow and Ajmer by the Indian Army to enable them to see the rest of India. They had gone beyond Srinagar for the first time in their lives. It was a great exposure for them to meet APJ Abdul Kalam, see the Jama Masjid, Red Fort, Ajmer Sharif and Taj Mahal etc. In each place, the Army units looked after them and took them to all the places around. These boys would never forget this experience. They now knew how big India was and how it was developing.

As the meal started, I realised how much Kashmiris loved eating and feasting. They were rather amused at seeing how little their guest ate. Gradually they started started discussing the Kashmir issue[2].

---

[2] The Kashmir conflict is a territorial conflict between India and Pakistan which started just after partition of India in 1947. India's claim on the State is based on an instrument of accession signed in 1947 between India and the then Maharaja of J&K. Pakistan wanted it, based on its majority Muslim population. Torn between the two emerging nations, the then King wanted a free, independent kingdom of J&K. India and Pakistan have fought three wars over Kashmir—the Indo-Pakistani Wars of 1947, 1965 and 1999. In 1947, Pakistan sent insurgents to wrest Kashmir valley from India, but this attempt was defeated by the people of Kashmir, assisted by Indian troops. The resulting First Kashmir War lasted until 1948, when India sought resolution of the issue at the UN Security Council. Thus came into being the United Nations Commission for India and Pakistan (UNCIP), and the

A tall, bearded person looked towards me and said, 'Sahib we do not understand much about India or Pakistan. The LoC has separated our families and friends. I have not met my uncles, aunts and cousins who are on the other side. I want to be free to go over to them and meet them whenever I want to. This is the essence of what we all want. You tell me is there anything wrong in our simple expectations?'

Another young teenage boy said, 'I want to study. To do so, I need to go out of Kashmir, wherever I can get admission. I want to earn money and live a better life. There is no future here. Only politics, pettiness and conspiracy seem to be present. We live very dangerously. Even Allah can't help us here.'

A prominent school teacher, Amanullah, stood up and said, 'Sir, we need to interact with you all more. We have so many problems in the Tangdhar valley. Srinagar does not care for these remote areas like ours. We are told that lot of money comes from Delhi for Kashmir. We never see or feel this money. Where does it go? What is our future? Our hearts cry out whenever an artillery gun fires. If the Indian Artillery fires towards PoK, we cry because our relatives in the villages across will get hurt. If the Pakistani Artillery fires at us, we cry out of fear for ourselves. Our land of Kashmir seems to be accursed.'

Hearing the school teacher Amanullah speak, an old Hindi film song, from my childhood days in late 1950s, came flashing to my mind:

UN Security Council passed Resolution 47 on 21 April 1948, which called for a plebiscite after an immediate ceasefire. From then on, Pakistan says, Kashmiris want a plebiscite. India says, Kashmir is part of India's democratic fabric and is open to election of its State government. In 1954, India subsequently issued a special law, the Constitution (Application to J& K) Order under Article 370 of the Indian Constitution, extending the Union Constitution to the State. However, this Order provided for some exceptions and modifications, which are bones of contention for the rest of India. Since 1984, India and Pakistan have also been involved in several skirmishes over control of the Siachen Glacier. As of today, India controls about 47 per cent of the land area including most of Jammu, the Kashmir valley and Ladhak while Pakistan occupies 37 per cent (Pok), calling it Azad Kashmir and the northern areas of Gilgit-Baltistan. China claims the Shaksam Valley and Aksai Chin. Elections to the J&K legislative assembly were held in December 2014, with more than 65 per cent voter turnout despite terrorist threats.

I am a rickshaw puller, a rickshaw puller,
My two feet make for four wheels of the rickshaw …
Why is there so much shortage of everything in this world ?
Who has stolen all these things, where is it all hidden ?

While much might have changed for the positive in India since 1950s, many basic issues relating to corruption and the governance deficit had only become worse.

Some were very forthright in accepting the fact that their leaning towards Pakistan was more natural, as the LoC had divided their families forever. Beyond this region, they did not have any affinity for the Punjabi-dominated Pakistan, which was dangerous and unpredictable. They were aware that democracy in India was a major plus point. Finally, the host realised that I did not have the mandate to answer all such questions, despite all my efforts to do so.

Then Mujib got up to speak. He thanked all of us for accepting the invitation and stated, 'After partition, we Kashmiris were quite content to be part of India. Sheikh Abdullah Sahib, our wise leader, decided that it is better for Kashmiris to be part of India and we agreed. It was the Maharaja of Kashmir who thought otherwise then. In the 1965 war, we did not support Pakistan who tried to infiltrate forces into Kashmir. In 1971, we did not support Pakistan. Till 1986, Kashmir was more peaceful than the entire North East India, Bihar or Punjab.'

Mujib looked around and saw others listening to him raptly. He continued. 'Sahib, you told me you were in Khrew, near Srinagar in 1976. Many times you used to drive into Lal Chowk at night to eat kebabs, fish fries and biryani with your families, without any fear. You also went to Pahalgam with your wife, along with other Army officers and their wives, to trek up the nearby mountains and spend nights in villages. You all used to take leave and roam around the beautiful Kashmir valley. You did so without any fear. You showed me your album full of black and white photographs. Sahib, tell me did we behave like *gaddars* or foreigners?'

I shook my head and said, 'not at all. We used to get into the apple orchards with our small children on our shoulders, pluck apples and eat them. We used to get into horse-driven carts with our wives and drive them along a stretch of the Srinagar-Baramula Road singing Hindi film songs. Local people used to watch us and laugh indulgently.'

Mujib smiled and looked towards everybody. The ex-MLA was making full use of his opportunities. He asked, 'If this was how life here was in 1976 and up to about 1986, what happened to Kashmir thereafter, that our beautiful valley lost its happiness forever? Who stoked the fire of hell in our land? Don't you realise that we have to ask ourselves such questions? Is it only Pakistan that is to blame? All the evil that has consumed us lies in the triangle formed by Delhi, Islamabad and Srinagar. *Khuda na kare ki yeh teenon hastiyan iss aag mein jhulas ke barbad ho jaye.* (God forbid these three entities get subsumed in this fire of their creation.)'

I thought over Mujib's comments. From then on, I increased my interactions with the locals of Tangdhar. I tried to win the hearts and minds of the locals. The Brigade used its own resources to repair some local schools, build some toilets, particularly for girl students in schools, organise computer training for children and repair some mosques which were not in a good state. The Army Engineer detachments built some micro-water projects and medical teams visited some remote villages to treat elderly patients who could not move out of their houses. So much could be done by making small efforts with available Army resources. Even providing a few cricket bats, balls, gloves and pads to the local children would bring such joy to them in those remote areas.

Why didn't governance touch their lives? Why didn't Srinagar feel their pain? Why did politics dominate governance so completely, especially in a region which was of such strategic importance for India? I felt miserable and frustrated on such issues. Of course, I was aware that a simplistic analysis tended to break down the complex issues in black and white, whereas the major grey shades of the Kashmir issue were far more intriguing and ominously strategic.

I completed a very meaningful tenure and was posted to Delhi. On my way out of the Tangdhar Valley, the helicopter carrying me was crossing over the narrow Nasta Chun Pass on the Pir Panjal ranges. The tenuous mountain road from Kupwara to Tangdhar went through this Pass. This windy pass is also called Sadhana Pass by the troops, after the famous and petite Bollywood actress Sadhana. An old large black and white photograph of the actress, well framed, is kept at the Army post there. I directed the smart, young helicopter pilot to fly over the valley once more. He flew over the neighbouring ridge lines enclosing the valley, which were held by the numerous posts strung all along the LoC, with moist eyes. His tears were for the gallant troops and junior officers who spend over two full years all on their own, in close proximity of Pakistani posts, braving the extreme weather, heights and enemy fire where any slackness could result in a widow and shattered families. Always cheerful, full of *josh* and proud of the fact that they were directly responsible for ensuring that Tangdhar Valley in India is always secure, they were the true sons of India, always ready and willing to do so much for so little. I solemnly saluted them and offered a silent prayer. I realised that there were tears in my eyes. I recollected the childhood song which had moved me to tears in late 1950s.

Jaago tumko baapu ki jagir ki raksha karni hai,
Jaago laakhon logon ki taqdeer ki raksha karni hai,
Abhi abhi jo bani hai us tasveer ki raksha karni hai,
Hoshiar tumko apni Kashmir ki raksha karni hai,
Saari duniya jal uthti hai muthi bhar angaron se,
Sambhal ke rahna apne ghar mein chhupe hue gaddaron se.

COUNTER-TERRORISM

A Conundrum called Kashmir

All countries in the world are territories of evil.

—Lord Rama

Within barely two years of posting at Delhi, I, on promotion as Major General, was posted as General Officer Commanding of a Counter-Terrorism Force in Jammu and Kashmir. The force had over fifteen thousand troops and officers. Within a month of my arrival, 9/11 took place[3]. It was a perilous and tense period, with two nuclear-armed nation closest to an all-out war. The main provocation which cracked India's patience was, of course, the Parliament attack by terrorists, planned and executed by Pakistan. A nuclear-armed nation, Pakistan, where its Army actually held power as well as the nuclear button, had severely and dangerously tested

[3] The 11 September attacks (also referred to as 9/11) were a series of four coordinated terrorist attacks by the Islamic terrorist group al-Qaeda on the United States on the morning of 11 September 2001. The suicide attacks targetted symbolic US landmarks like the World Trade Centre in New York city and the Pentagon building in Washington. Four passenger airliners—which all departed from airports on the US East Coast bound for California—were hijacked by nineteen al-Qaeda terrorists to be flown into these buildings. As many as 2,996 people died and over 6,000 were injured in the attacks.

democratic nuclear-armed India yet again, where civil supremacy existed and an elected government under the Prime Minister held the nuclear button.

How can two nuclear-armed countries find a window for a limited conventional war and yet achieve a victory, without escalating into nuclear weapons dimension? No one knew the answer or anything about such a threshold, about such an epic boundary, a *Lakshman Rekha.* Both the militaries were in eyeball-to-eyeball deployment. This was now no longer an Indo-Pak issue but a global problem.

The terrible event of 9/11 created a lot of euphoria among the Kashmiris on both sides of the LoC. This was a classic example of 'Irrational Exuberance'. It spread the contagious illusion that the American and European powers will wilt and global Jihad will engulf the world. Back to twelfth century. People from some parts of the world, who felt they had no hope, drank into this contagion of distorted ideas and theories.

The scale and intensity of terrorism assumed serious impetus soon after. Hundreds of trained, brain-washed or rather brain-dirtied terrorists in small groups started infiltrating across the most difficult terrain of the LoC from Akhnoor in the south, to Kargil in the north. Clashes between terrorist groups and the Army took place almost on a daily basis. Over fifty terrorists were being killed every month along this vast stretch of LoC and interior regions. Indian troops also suffered regular casualties. Encounters were intense, heavily fought out. Terrorists were highly trained, ready to die. Many were looking forward to die as long as they caused enough damage in that endeavour. Apart from deep-rooted religious indoctrination, there was economics involved.

Pakistan has an elaborate policy of credible monetary compensation. Fixed amount of money are paid regularly to the families of terrorists in Pakistan. Amounts are specified for successful infiltration, duration of stay inside India, for killing security forces, troops, officers, killing of Kashmiris who dare to display closeness to security forces, suicidal attacks on Indian detachments in the hinterland etc. These cash awards are regularly, without fail sent to the families. The terrorists are all educated in selected Madarsas in

Pakistan, where only fundamentalism and extreme interpretations of religion are taught. This renders them incapable of any other employability but terrorism. The terrorists are young, hot blooded, capable of intense raw cruelty, adventurists. As long as they live, they live like lords of all they survey on the Indian side of Kashmir. Back home in their villages, their families are well provided for by Pakistan. This is done quite honestly in Pakistan, which is flush with foreign cash given for this very purpose from the richest region of the Islamic world. Such are the devious games nations play.

Luckily for India, the Indian Armed Forces are blessed with excellent soldiers, sons of the soil of rural, semi-urban India, fashionably called Bharat by eminent educated urban Indians. Such professional soldiers are very ably led by well-trained and motivated junior officers at the level of Captains and Majors. Sadly enough, only a few of them go on to become battalion, regimental commanders as Colonels and above. These are the levels at which counter-terrorism operations are fought. Therefore, the strongest links in the chain of Indian Armed Forces structure are pitted against the terrorists who themselves are very well trained and highly motivated.

I, as a General Officer commanding my widely-deployed force, understood this reality and witnessed with great pride, the display of valour and patriotism of my troops and officers. I tried to support them, acknowledge their services and hold their hands during adverse situations. Practically every month, I had to absorb the harsh realities of my own troops and officers being killed or wounded in the process of neutralising scores of foreign terrorists, killed during encounters. They just would not surrender. Civil society in India is not fully aware of the sacrifices of its soldiers, their fierce nationalism, dedication to preserve the entity of India and its unity. If it was so aware, it would care more about its Army.

Conduct of national elections in such a disturbed region is indeed a phenomenal feat, accomplished by India's strongest, ablest institution, the Election Commission. It is quite amazing to have such institutions in a country of very sub-standard governance. I felt proud of the various government officials daring to go to the remotest villages, climbing hills, through jungles, with voting machines, braving dangers from terrorists who were hell bent to disrupt elections. The Indian Army, though not directly involved in the elections, had to sanitise large areas by dominating the entire sector with intense patrolling and area domination. It was a great responsibility, undertaken with dedication to protect these helpless civil officials accompanied by few ill-trained, ill-equipped, but brave policemen.

Most locals wanted to exercise their democratic right to vote for a suitable candidate, especially after they had borne the brunt of bad governance. The terrorists had threatened them and obstructed them from voting. Locals wanted the security forces to visibly force them to vote, so that they could tell the vengeful terrorists that they were forced to vote. It was not possible to accede to this request. I, however, allowed them to give this excuse to save themselves, to those who got into such a situation, while ensuring that extensive operations are on covering the entire area so that terrorists were confined to their high mountain hideouts. Democratic India has every reason to be proud of the Kashmiris who braved grave dangers to vote for candidates who, hopefully, would provide better governance. But alas!

The Jammu and Kashmir police live dangerously, particularly those who are deployed in remote districts and tehsils. Some of them suffer casualties. Every elected government of the State owes a lot to these policemen. They deserve to be better trained, equipped, housed and led. Finally, they should be enabled to take on the terrorists beyond the confines of Srinagar. In the global context, in whichever country, the police forces are handling terrorists and secessionist elements, it is largely perceived as an internal problem. When regular Army handles internal security for too long, it is seen globally as an international problem. The problem in India is that its State police are quite pathetic, neglected, ill-equipped, sans good leadership, ill-trained and reasonably potbellied. This is an important characteristic of a typically third world nation.

One day, I visited the most sensitive locality of the general area Rajouri-Poonch, known as Surankote. The Brigadier controlling the general area was a busy man indeed. Terrorism and militancy was deeply embedded in this sector. He had fixed up an interaction with local community leaders and MLAs, ex MLAs at the High School of Surankote. It was a Sunday. The locals preferred such meetings in their midst, rather than being called into the military campus, usually located on dominating ground around the village.

A small group of a dozen Kashmiris were seated inside the school. Four important people were seated in the centre. They were to be the ones who would be speaking. Mohammed Ghani was the MLA, Rasool was the previous MLA, Maqsood was an educated, elderly gentleman who owned large tracts of land in Surankote. The local Maulvi was a very influential person in Surankote.

The customary welcome speech was longer than desired, but such local formalities had to be endured. The local Kashmiri leaders were very efficient in delivering lectures. Every aspect of their conversation had to be heard intently, as there were deeper meaning to some of the things they mentioned. All such meetings, interaction had specific agendas, well thought out, well rehearsed.

After the formalities were done, cups of tea went around. Ghani started the interaction.

'General Sahib, the Army here is rendering lots of help to us in many aspects of our daily lives. Operation Sadbhavna, as you call it, is very effective. Our *mubarak* to you for this. The students of Surankote and the schools are receiving lots of help from the Army. The medical facilities extended by you all are a big help. However, the intensity of military operation are at a high pitch. This causes problems at times.'

I responded. 'We shall not only continue with our Sadhbavna projects but also find more ways to undertake small projects to help the locals in various other ways. We plan to take fifteen high school boys on a trip to Delhi, Ajmer, Hyderabad and Bangalore. I am told that the boys here have never crossed Jammu in their lives so far. They will get exposed to what all are happening in India and now feel positive. We shall conduct training camps in computers for the students.'

'However, intensity of operation is directly related to enhanced infiltration of terrorists from Pakistan. Having violence-free environment is critical to peace and prosperity. For this, we need your cooperation. All those who enter India from Pakistan without visas, but with weapons and explosives, do not do so to solve your problems. They come here for their own agendas which harm us all. Please remember this.'

The Maulvi now entered the discussion.

'Sir, see the larger picture. Islam arrived in Kashmir in 1323 when it expanded worldwide. A local saint, Bul Bul Sha first converted to Islam and initiated mass conversions. He was teacher to the ruler Rinchan, also known as Malik Sadar-ud-Din (1323-1326). Later this king was killed by Kashmiris. Kashmir lies along the routes which invaders took to capture India. We bore the brunt then also. Allah gave us such a beautiful area but human history gave us constant subjugations and misery, up to this day.

'Sir, see the larger picture today. As much as forty five per cent of our Kashmir is under India, thirty five per cent under Pakistan and twenty per cent is claimed by China. Until 1947, Kashmir was free from both India and Pakistan. There is an Indian perspective on Kashmir, there is a Pakistan perspective and now a godless China perspective. Who cares about the Kashmiri perspective? We are nothing. Everyone views us from their own narrow perspectives and call us *gaddars*. No one understands the existential dilemma of Kashmir. Why can't Kashmir be a global zone of peace and let us live, without India and Pakistan, but under international jurisdiction? Sir, I know what I am saying is much beyond the capabilities of India, Pakistan or China. The rest of humanity, globalised world has to take charge.'

Rasool joined in. 'Sir, we agree with you. We too are defenceless victims of terrorism. Sir, Kashmiris need to be better understood. Our social structure in the valley and here is based on the *Biradari* concept. Biradari means brotherhood. We Kashmiris lived isolated historically. We are introverts. Our understanding of collective security and well being is exclusively within our *Biradari*. Kashmiri *Biradari* has been geographically separated between India and Pakistan part of our Kashmir. Our uncles and relatives are on the other side too. Sir, the rest of India and non-Kashmir Pakistan need to understand this.'

Maqsood interjected, 'Sir, please appreciate the fact that because we benefit so much from the Army, we are close enough to each other to speak frankly. Hence do not misunderstand us. We cannot speak so frankly with our political leaders based in Srinagar. The Army and local people together face a tough life here in Kashmir.

'While India and Pakistan battle with each other with guns, bullets, terrorism and counter-terrorism, the masses of Kashmiris in distant regions and villages battle with insecurity, fear, identity confusion, poverty, illiteracy, no hope for the young generation, lack of governance, corruption etc. We are like wheat grains pressed between the grinder.'

I thought I needed to balance the discussion. 'Gentlemen, you all were young boys when India got independence and it took the secular approach. Tell me honestly. Did you not enjoy playing around freely amidst these beautiful *wadis,* the hills, rivers, springs. There were no interferences in your lives. Rest of India suffered so much during the horrible partition period. Then why have you all created conditions that your children, grandchildren are suffering due to extremism? Aren't you all also responsible for being misled due to seeing everything from the prism of religion? The entire world cannot be partitioned, based only on religion. Please realise that we are human beings first, religions came much later. We have entered the 21st century and cannot go eight centuries backwards. This is also a basic fact, without which we can never comprehend the larger picture.

'You all hear about Army atrocities elsewhere in Kashmir from the press, media and deliberately planted, false or exaggerated rumours. Army is here in large numbers in the vast hinterland of the Rajouri–Poonch region where you all live. When have we done atrocities on you all? Yet, wrong rumours are spread against us. At times, yes, we carry out operations only to intercept and neutralise those who come here from Pakistan to conduct terrorist attacks. Ask the Bangladeshis, what happened to them from 1969 to 1971. Then you get another larger picture.

'You all know what I am talking about. So, our discussions on your problems should be more honest, more truthful. We all are equally sensitive to all the genuine problems and dilemmas faced by you. Tell me, do not the rural people in India, Pakistan, Bangladesh or any other country face so many problems? Solving problems of governance, corruption, poverty, unemployment are constant issues which need to be corrected. In that aspect, we are all with you. Your hearts and minds, your votes, your resentment against poor governance must be ignited towards the correct issues. Do not fiddle with the future of your coming generation and show the younger generation the wrong route and spread false perspectives in their young minds.'

Now Ghani very promptly changed the flow of the discussion to mundane day-to-day issues, where the Army could do more. He talked about skill development training for locals, sponsoring of some of them for going to Srinagar, Jammu for courses in polytechnics, problems of sickness of cattle as there was no veterinary doctors, problems of Gujjars who have to take their animals into the forest for months for grazing, shortage of good teachers in schools etc. The meeting ended with smiles and hugs. MLA Ghani as well as ex-MLA Rasool were very active in trying to outshine each other. I allowed them to do so.

That evening I pondered over all this. The Hurriyat is an alliance of twenty-six political, social and religious organisation formed in 1993 to propagate Kashmiri separatism and Pakistan's unfinished agenda after partition. Its primary role is to defame Indian counter-insurgency and anti-terrorism operations. They know that it is only the Indian Army, which is capable of preventing independence of Kashmir at first, so it could join Pakistan later. In this endeavour, the Hurriyat faces fissures within its own organisation.

The reality is that serious geopolitical interests of India and Pakistan merge in Kashmir. For India, it is the symbol of its secular existence. For Pakistan, it is the symbol of its origin, the jugular vein of its two-nation theory, despite its own breakup of East Pakistan in 1971. Now, after 1998, Kashmir is wedged between the triad of three nuclear-armed states of India, Pakistan and China. Add to this the religious fundamentalism in Afghanistan, Tibet, Central Asia Republics, Xingxian province of China and the entire North West expanse of China. The cauldron is extremely complicated. Will Kashmir ever graduate as a global zone of peace? Is any part of the globe as strategically significant, a zone of peace?

I also thought about the three perspectives on Kashmir. The Indian and Pakistani perspectives in Kashmir, however antagonistic they may be mutually, are clear and amply stated. Then there is the Chinese perspective of land grab. The Kashmiri perspective is ambiguous, confused, cloaked in a different agenda on which there is no unanimity not only amongst Kashmiris in the valley but also with Kashmiris of the Jammu region and Ladakh.

The strategic position of Kashmir is such that without it, Pakistan cannot defend itself against India, towards which it seems to have decided to always remain in confrontational mode. Neither can Pakistan threaten India militarily, without Kashmir.

There are three out of the six rivers which originate in Kashmir—the Indus, Jhelum and Chenab flow into Pakistan. So Jammu and Kashmir remains one of the most militarised zones in the world.

The best road ahead is to rule out any prospect of war between India and Pakistan. A state of near-parity in military terms appears to be the main obstacle. For this, India has to share the largest blame. For the last seventy years after India's independence, its governance, its development, its economy has performed much below its potential. Hence, India is just a big power in South Asia, the most impoverished region of Asia. This is not saying much.

There are many global problems for which no solutions seem imminent. Kashmir will remain one of them till India rises to its true potential in economic terms, till its development pace, quality of delivery of governance and its own nation-building processes take a quantum leap. India must leave Pakistan as much behind as India is presently lagging behind China. Just as India will not be able to initiate a proactive war with China, Pakistan must also be unable to challenge India militarily. Indian civilisation has never conquered other countries and still remains so. Pakistan and rest of the world understand this well. When India progresses that much—as it should anyway—Kashmiris will know what is in their best interest. Simultaneously, when relations between India and China become more strategic and economic as part of the imminent rise of Asia, many contentious issues of today will reach their logical conclusions. There is a long waiting period ahead.

Every night I realised that up to a thousand men of my force were out on operations, for dominating the areas by their surreptitious presence, based on various intelligence inputs of likely movement of groups of terrorists. The area was mountainous, jungle-clad up to heights on which trees grew (treeline), thereafter rugged, barren up to over fifteen thousand feet at places. Many natural caves, ravines, gorges etc littered the tough, unforgiving landscape. Tiny hamlets, villages existed in narrow valleys and hill-tops. Larger villages were located at lower heights and broader valleys. It was easy for terrorists to hide their weapons and merge with the locals so that Army patrols could not identify them. A few kilometres away from the villages, on dominating grounds, some local lookout persons could easily hide and watch the movements of Army columns and report their activities to the village, to enable terrorists to get away. Any failure to do so would result in severe reprisals by the terrorists.

Encounters, which took place when Army columns, by using good tactics and moving along most inaccessible areas, could surprise the terrorists, were very fiercely resisted. Usually, encounters continued for many hours, at times for over twelve hours, till the last of the terrorists were eliminated. There would also be casualties to Indian troops and officers. Daring helicopter pilots would fly in their machines on hill-tops, wherever a small clearing was available to evacuate the casualties. Before that, the area had to be well sanitised and cleared of terrorists to ensure safety of the helicopters. During every such operation, I prayed hard and deep. Things can go wrong with catastrophic results. The junior officers, the troops, their battalion commander's jobs were far more stressful and risk-prone. They needed all the luck. The terrorists, in any case, came from across the border to kill and die in the process. When such foreign-based, lethally-armed terrorists infiltrate from a neighbouring country and take on the regular Army, it is War. This is THE WAR of the 21st Century. This is the war which is waged unofficially against a country that has created an adverse situation on its own soil due to lack of good governance and due to dominance of poor politics over nation-building.

During one such major encounter, a large group of terrorists were successfully entrapped in a dense mountain region. I was informed about the commencement of the encounter at around midnight. The entire operations room of my Headquarters was activated immediately. Detail of all aspects was being passed on from the Brigade HQ, under which the encounter was taking place. Major Sibal was leading the operation. He was a daring officer, who always led from the front in a couple of operations earlier. He informed his Battalion and Brigade Commander that the group of terrorists entrapped had crossed the LoC in small groups, and had regrouped at a rendezvous five kilometres inside India, when they were detected by the small Indian surveillance party. Major Sibal had rushed to the area with reinforcements and had surrounded the group. A fierce encounter was on. It was difficult to close in due to darkness and any move to close in was being heard due to slippery terrain.

The fire-fight was getting into a situation of stalemate and Major Sibal reported that soon the terrorists would try to slip out of the cauldron individually. So, with a small group of soldiers, he said he would creep closer to the terrorists and surprise them. Now I became concerned. I asked the Brigade Commander to tell Maj Sibal not to try such a risky move and to increase the volume of high trajectory fire and illumination to get as many of them as he could. The operation can continue over next few days, with other units encircling larger areas. But, by then, the brave Major Sibal had already switched off his communication set. He had taken his decision. Next morning I got the report that Major Sibal was among the fatal casualties of our troops with four more wounded. Such are the calibre of junior officers in the Army. Eight terrorists were killed. One of them was prominent and a deadly regional commander. There were many such cases of heroic officers and men fighting deadly battles to stop foreign terrorists from creating mayhem and destabilising Kashmir seriously.

By now, I had a deeper, mature understanding of Kashmir. I had interacted with Kashmiris at grassroots level, understood their predicaments, their follies, their complexities borne out of centuries of existence in a region which bore the initial brunt of conquerors, from Alexander to the ruthless Mughal forces rampaging towards hinterland India. Subjugations after subjugations sowed the embryonic seeds of intense desire for being the master of their own lives. Nature always bestowed its best on this beautiful land, but it was cursed by geography which made this land too strategic for comfort.

The kaleidoscopic sequence of global history crossed this region and continues to do so in the 21st Century too. In the 21st Century, we all hope for a better future and insist it must be better still. For many people living in this largely modern, scientific, democratic, liberalised world, future is still remote. Yet, they too feel they have a bright future. Till the less fortunate see light of hope, the world can never be peaceful. Bulk of the population of South Asia have the right to go on hoping for a better future. Of course, there are no easy remedies. Peace between India and Pakistan is the best remedy, just as peace in Europe was the only remedy. Britain, France and Germany managed to attain it, but only after slaughtering each other for centuries. India and Pakistan does not have that luxury of time.

The 21st Century is a century of innovations, of a flatter world. Every type of innovation are being created, economic, scientific, business, social engineering etc. Political innovation is the only one lagging behind. Perhaps the worst of human resources are in this field in most nations.

There have been numerous occasions since 1990 to date, I recollected, when intense, successful military anti-terrorist operations brought stability in Kashmir. These were achieved at the cost of a lot of casualties and sacrifices. Lakhs of tourists from the hinterland of Indian and abroad started pouring in. Locals started earning money. Jobs were created. There were smiles in the enchanting valley. The beautiful valley was the first choice of young couples on honeymoon. This Kashmir valley was created by God for love making, not for war waging. Unfortunately, never were serious attempts made—neither by the Central government, nor by the State government—to consolidate on the prevailing stability. On the contrary, petty politics, corruption, infighting for political space rose during such periods. Opportunities for resolving people's grievances and ensuring responsive governance were missed. Soon, many such periods of stability degenerated into return of terrorism and fresher impetus from across the border and LoC.

Kashmiris are cursed with leadership deficit. More or less the same deficiency has been visible in much of South Asia. Keeping South Asia forever subjugated and underdeveloped seems to be the predominant death wish of India and Pakistan.

In the bargain, two of the finest military forces in the world are interlocked in a mutually-assured destruction dance. If these two militaries combine together, terrorism will wither from South Asia as well as Afghanistan. What a stupid dream to dream, I thought. That too at a time when a conventional war between the two countries seemed imminent in 2001. 'Com'on you idiot, you are tired and getting old', I said to myself. 'Come back to real world, and the retirement which is just about four years away. No active tenures till then any more. The old order changeth, yielding place to the new.'

At the end of my tenure, I was posted to Army War College at Mhow in Madhya Pradesh. Both the tenures in Jammu and Kashmir were challenging and stressful and I looked forward to the peaceful, academic environment of the fine training institution at Mhow. I could now pay more attention to my children. I now wanted to spend much more time with my wife. I hadn't even decided where to settle down on retirement, a fact which worried me now. 'Have I let down my wife on this score?' I wondered.

One year before retirement, on return from an official tour to Israel, I suffered a complicated heart attack. I was physically so fit, never, ever got admitted in a hospital, was not a smoker, never overindulged in life. 'Why me?' I gasped. Always a *Ram Bharose-* (depend upon God-) type of a person, I felt that God, who had been protective towards me all along, would continue to do so forever. I also had the conviction that God's benevolence in the unforeseen, uncharted, largely unplanned life after retirement would continue. Now I was a bit shaky.

BATTLE WITHIN

Superpower and People's Protests

To be a saint is the exception, to be upright is the rule. Err, falter, sin, but be upright. To commit the least possible sin is the law for man. The guilty one is not he who commits the sin, but the one who causes the darkness.

—Victor Hugo

As the inevitable retirement drew closer, I hoped to work in the corporate sector. I thought my life would be incomplete if I did not experience how life is outside the uniformed, exclusive world. I also felt the need to build a house at a place where we could lead a peaceful and happy retired life. To do this, I needed to work for a while more. To retire and do nothing at the age of fifty-eight was not desirable. Meanwhile, I had completed my Doctorate in Management.

On retirement, I got an offer to be an Advisor, Community Development Projects as part of Rehabilitation and Resettlement for a hydro-electric project on the Narmada river in Madhya Pradesh, the Shree Maheshwar Hydel Power Corporation Ltd. I promptly accepted this offer. Thus started a new learning process in experiencing the complexities and struggles of people uprooted by to submergence of many villages due to a hydro-electric dam. My dilemma about conflicts, both external and internal, increased even more as my conviction that lack of good governance led to conflicts was reaffirmed.

On one side was the developmental need of hydroelectric energy for a nation's growing economy. On the other side were the villagers, whose villages had to get submerged as a price to be paid for the nation's insatiable, limitless need for energy.

In a nation where the quality of governance was so abysmally sub-standard, how could one deliver a good and efficient Rehabilitation and Resettlement package? I knew that I was again getting into a very serious, complex, conflict-prone situation, albeit of an entirely different kind. I would now get a shocking grassroots experience of how villages, Panchayats, Blocks, Tehsils and Districts really function in the Bharat part of India, the largest democracy in the world, selling the dream of becoming a superpower to its gullible people. Linkages between lack of governance, disconnect of the rulers with the pain, anguishes of helpless villagers and Naxalism soon became obvious.

The hydro-electric project was under the management of highly able engineers, technicians and experts. Therefore, the technical aspects of the project were well taken care of. However, such an able, competent team of engineers and experts lacked matching competence in dealing with agitated, at times violent, villagers whose centuries-old villages and way of life were about to be drowned under the catchment area of the dam. The Project-Affected People (PAP) felt cheated and betrayed by the State government, suspicious of the manner in which it had negotiated the project with a private company. This was their perception as well as their conviction. I was now actually experiencing the saying, '*Yeh public hai, sab jaanti hai.* (This is the public, they know everything.)'

The villagers had no faith in the honest delivery of Rehabilitation and Resettlement package by the government and the private firm combine. The anti-dam activists of the Narmada Bachaao Andolan and other sister organisations were extremely active in providing leadership and channelising of the angst and deep resentment of the affected villages. Initially, I was told how these activists were 'obstructing India's progress' and its industrialisation by misguiding the simple villagers into use of 'anti-national' methods.

Somehow, civil society and the corporate world have no idea about the range and depth of knowledge military officers acquire on a vast number of issues such as India's strength and weaknesses, quality of governance, non-inclusive growth, neglect of rural India, corruption, low level politics and many other ground realities, both negative and positive ones. After all, soldiers also come from the same Bharat and all the complex problems encountered by them in their villages are known to the officers for three to four decades of the duration of their service.

Just as a chain is as strong as its weakest link, India is only as strong as Bharat or rural India is. In fact, from Kashmir to the North East, Bihar or UP, a person in every State of India up to Cape Comorin, across the length and width of India suffers bad governance and mean politics. However, in spite of this, the fact that India still continues to survive, do well globally in other spheres of activities, has a pulsating democracy, is a marvel of human endeavour and achievements.

Development projects in rural India get involved in this melee and tend to lose their way. The hearts and minds of the people have to be won not only in Kashmir or North East, but everywhere. This is the essence of democracy after all. This is not the job of technicians, scientists and professional experts only. This is the job of governance, the weakest link in the chain called India. To complicate matters more, this link is also the most arrogant, ruthless and a rootless one. While pondering over all this, my mind was full of trepidation.

A retired Army Lt Colonel, named A K Singh, was directly dealing with the intricacies of Rehabilitation and Resettlement Policy for the project. He was working very hard indeed. The top brass located at Delhi and Mumbai were only too willing to outsource their moral, ethical, professional, commitments and social responsibilities towards the poor and highly-politicised people, affected by the project. So this competent, hardworking, retired Lt Colonel was bearing the brunt of local resistance. His mission was a thankless one.

I noticed that while the top management of the project had a clear vision and plans for the construction of the dam, there appeared to be no serious commitment, vision, empathy and availability of adequate funds for compensating the affected villagers. There were laid down the minimum of rehabilitation—which had to be done legally as per the policy framed by the Government of India and the State—which itself was disputed by the locals as 'unfair', both in their content and execution.

The intent of abiding by the spirit of the Rehabilitation policy and its correct, qualitative implementation on the ground was not there. Aspects of Resettlement suffered from similar malaise. It is well-known that the spirit and aim of any business is to maximise profits, create wealth with minimum resources. This very limited understanding of business keeps third world countries for ever third class countries.

The anti-dam activities, at the working level, were more in the business of opposing the dam itself rather than on monitoring the implementation of the Rehabilitation and Resettlement. The ideal aim of the activists should have been to allow progression of such an essential development project as well as ensure that the project-affected villagers got a fair deal, which would ensure that in their new resettled areas, their quality of life was at least a shade better than before.

This was what I thought initially. Later on, I would realise that nothing in India is quite so simple. In fact, I found everything about Resettlement and Rehabilitation was rather dubious and devious. In about a year's time, I realised that rural India requires social activists and NGOs who stand up against injustice. They make democracy grow in strength. I also understood that such activists and NGOs should also remain under close scrutiny, as they too tend to go haywire with their activism. Initially, they are led by motivated leaders. Soon, such leaders grow in stature and get globalised. Those who replace them may not be as good.

However, I was confident that all experiences of Operation Sadbhavana in Kashmir and North East would help me to do some useful work here. Doing something which will help suffering people is a moral, social and spiritual call. I also sincerely wished that important, critical development projects succeed in meeting the energy requirements of a backward, impoverished, malnourished State like Madhya Pradesh.

The Indian Army executes multifarious welfare projects in insurgency-and terrorist-affected areas called Operation Sadbhavana, with its own resources. Various micro-projects like building schools, equipping schools, opening health centres, water projects, mini power projects, roads, rural electrification, livelihood enhancing projects, skill training are implemented. Students are sponsored, given exposure to all that is happening in the rest of the country. Tuitions and such other innovative methods to help the people are adopted. Such micro-projects have macro impact in showing the human face of the Army. They also serve as a band aid in reducing the pain of governance deficit. In fact, in such areas, people start approaching the Army for grievance redressal rather than go to government institutions, which is not desirable. So the Army interacts with district-level government institutions. Wherever such institutions are headed by efficient, well-intentioned civil service officials, a lot of improvement takes place. In such an environment, terrorists, insurgents find it very difficult to undertake violent actions. Dilution of local support is anathema to anti-national elements. They get eliminated faster. Those Army units, which do not realise the relevance of Operation Sadbhavana, encounter major problems, commit grave errors and fail to serve the nation properly.

There are few problems in economic development, as contentious as land acquisition. Yet, an economically resurgent India, with its large-scale manufacturing ambitions, needs to acquire land. This is an era of vast industries which need vast amount of contiguous lands. How does one put a value to a piece of land which will produce food and sustain a family for generations, for ages? Agriculture is not only an industry by itself, but also a way of life. So the inevitable questions are asked. Development for whom? At whose costs? Who all are the stakeholders and who are not? Laws are made by those who rule. Those who rule are those who control power in India.

So laws are, at times, made for obedience by the weak and to serve the interests of the strong. The strong can always exploit windows of opportunity to beat the system. However, the strong are eminently predisposed to underestimating the anger of the masses. Greed was always considered good. Now it appears to be legal.

An industry like a hydro-electric project, which will create wealth perpetually, has to ensure that locals are stakeholders in the project. How to do that? Has the concept and spirit of Corporate Social Responsibility (CSR) matured yet in India? Does it only exist in the syllabus of Business Management Institutions, academically? Some wise, benign corporate houses are very sincere towards this endeavour and reap long-term benefits. Most corporates do not practice CSR, particularly in remote rural areas, thinking that local people are fools, which is far from the truth.

They are very aware, clever and have the power to stall any project. Spending tens of crores on their resettlement and livelihood would reduce loss of hundreds and thousands of crores due to delays and disruptions.

There are innovative, not-so-expensive ways in which the resettlement of the sacrificing villagers can be mitigated. There are a growing number of graduates from IITs and IIMs who are running their own NGOs and have great expertise on these issues. They do have viable solutions to such challenges by creating a win-win environment wherein NGOs also grow and the locals also benefit. I was convinced that an NGO must make fair profit as long as rural folks also benefit, more than hitherto. In this respect, such well-conceived and professionally well-managed NGOs offer a better deal to the locals than what most government institutions can ever do. This is the reality of India, the land of Karma.

The only officer who had the courage to go into all the affected villages, particularly those who were most opposed to the dam, was the Lt Colonel from the Army. This officer took risks. He came close to being beaten by villagers on some occasions. Others mostly preferred to remain in their offices. I accompanied him, to understand the ground realities.

In one such village, I met over a hundred-odd villagers who assembled near a temple in the centre of the village. I explained to them about some community development projects I was trying to work on. I had interacted with a corporate which was producing garments for export. The firm had hundreds of modern stitching machines, producing thousands of shirts, trousers and other clothing items based on firm export orders. The firm had agreed to train twenty boys from our project area for four months during which they would be paid a stipend, and later absorbed. They could, after training, earn about five thousand rupees per month. I also explained that the project management would soon start a skill imparting programme, wherein fifty boys of the affected villages would be trained in skills like electrician, wiremen, plumber, carpenter, mechanic, fitter etc. by the technicians based at the dam site.

For the women, I planned to purchase one hundred spinning machines which are manufactured in Gujarat. One such machine would be placed in each of the hundred houses, about ten in each village. A neighbouring Swiss NGO, working on encouraging many villagers to produce organic cotton, would train these women in spinning organic threads free of charge. They would provide organic cotton slivers free. The women would have to spin the threads while going about their domestic chores at home, whenever they managed the time. Twice a month, the threads would be weighed, collected and they would be paid in cash for their labour, depending on how much they produced from the machine. On an average, a woman could earn about three thousand rupees a month from this labour. This project had sound economic logic. The Swiss NGO had enormous orders for organic clothes like vests, under clothing, socks, gloves and shirts. This spinning activity was the first in the chain of activities which led on to weaving of clothes, certification of the organic products, labelling that these were produced by poor women from dam-affected villages in India, struggling to earn more to feed their children better. It was a classic win-win business model in which everyone made money. It was inclusive wealth creation. Poor village women, now earning three thousand rupees and more, while remaining at home with a machine placed free in their houses.

They only had to time-manage the daily chores, stop wasteful gossiping and work on the spinning machines and produce the spindles of organic thread.

Later on, I would encourage these women to form self-help groups (SHGs) which could avail micro-financing—loans—to collectively buy these machines and increase production, leading to increased earnings. Such a spinning machine was available for about eight thousand rupees. Other women could also form self-help groups, take small loans and start micro projects which would help them to improve their livelihood. For this, there was another NGO headed by a visionary person. He was educated at the Indian Institute of Technology, Delhi, Indian Institute of Management Ahmedabad and at the Princeton University, USA. I thought that this NGO could be utilised. It had vast knowledge and expertise with viable international linkages on rural livelihood projects. They ran Livelihood Schools all over the country.

As I was explaining to the villagers all my plans, one old village elder got up to speak. 'Respected General Sahib, we hear you; I have seen life and I can say you are a well-meaning, God-fearing person. You sound sincere. We appreciate what you are trying to do. But being a military man, you have no idea of the ruthlessness of the system in civil life. In uniform, you must have felt very proud of your country. Now you are out of uniform for a few months only. Very soon, you will be ashamed of your country at the reality of lack of justice and corruption that prevails here. You will not be able to continue in this job for long. You will not be permitted to implement these good plans you are making for us. You will be side-lined. You will not get the resources to do so. This dam is only going to evict us from our villages. We gain nothing from the electricity, which this dam is supposed to be producing. We will be forced out and relocated in the cheapest fashion somewhere else. There will be a fraudulent rehabilitation. There will be no resettlement. The only winner will be the corporate owner of the dam and government officials.'

The old man continued while all the villagers listened grimly. 'Listen, Sahib to what the Narbada river says as it flows peacefully towards the Arabian Sea. We have been listening to the flowing river since ancient times. Narbada Maa has cursed this dam. You are in the wrong place, on the wrong side of a class struggle.'

Finally he concluded very significantly, and with firm conviction, 'Sahib, I am older than you. I am uneducated and from a low caste. You have combated terrorism in Kashmir. I would like to tell you that terrorism does not exist only in Kashmir. Terrorism exists in most parts of rural and tribal India. Terrorism is there in mining activities, even in villages, land mafias, in some powerful politicians who own enormous land and have thugs employed to expand their wealth, in forest resources. It exists in backward Naxal-infested regions where the poor, the weak, affected by malnutrition suffer terrorism both from the democratic state and from the Naxalities. We do not live along borders with Pakistan. We are well inside India. We too suffer. Even bad governance is a form of terrorism due to the human sufferings it causes.'

I could fathom the rage which is becoming the dominant emotion in rural India. It is different from the rage of the middle class. This is rage seething within the underprivileged, of the indigent, of *Les Miserables* who see no hopes, no deliverance. For how long can this rage be controlled by the release valve of power to vote every few years! The rage of people who cannot defend themselves within the prevailing system. Amidst the ever-growing visible islands of arrogant prosperity, surrounded by oceans of those at the bottom of the social pyramid, people are angry.

I had a very fascinating interaction with two prominent anti-dam activists of the area, Alok Agarwal and Chitrarupa Palit. They were fiery, resolute and quite uncompromising in their views on the injustices being perpetuated on the villagers of this backward district due to the construction of this dam and provided leadership to the protest movement. There were also others like Sanjay and Nidhi. These two were in their early forties. I met them in one of the anti-dam villages. The Sarpanch of the village had invited me for lunch at his home as I had got delayed, moving around a few dusty villages in the vicinity. As I was ushered into the house, I saw the two activists sitting inside. We knew each other and hence, after formal greetings, we settled down. I realised that today, for the first time, I would be in a serious conversation amidst a more informal environment, with these two very professional activists. We settled down inside the room with glasses of *nimbupani* being refilled from time to time.

'So, General Sahib, tell me, are you satisfied with the pace and quality of R and R (Rehabilitation and Resettlement)?' Sanjay asked.

'Well, it is difficult to state that one is fully satisfied in executing such a complex and non-linear mission', I replied. 'However', I continued, 'it is worth a try.'

'Sir, I agree with and appreciate the first part of your answer. The layers of dust on your clothes and your tired, grimy face speak for itself. For the second part, we don't see you staying in this job for too long. You will soon quit. They will not allow you to do "anything". They are ruthless.'

'And why do you think so?' was my bemused response.

'Because, you do not fit into this corporate environment. Your grooming and training in life, your perceptions, thought processes, in fact, your entire persona is far too different from your employers, bureaucrats, politicians. You are not like them.'

I kept quiet and remained in a listening mode.

Nidhi took up the discussion from Sanjay. 'Sir, my late uncle was an Army Colonel. Therefore, I understand your future predicaments in the coming months. You feel that your experiences in handling the suffering people in insurgency-prone areas of North East and Kashmir will enable you to provide value additions to the moribund, insincerely-conceived R and R policy of the Centre and this corrupt State. General, while you were in service in such areas, you had the resources made available to you by the Army institutions in terms of military equipment, logistic units and disciplined, obedient manpower. There, it was based on formal military vision and plans, well-conceived, with commensurate resources allotted, well-blended with the military aspects of counter-insurgency operations. The rest of the country does not function with such clinical efficiency and sincerity of purpose. Welcome to the real India, General!'

I replied, 'But assuming, the fair element of reality check you are giving me is correct, are you all in any manner contributing towards correcting the flaws in the real India in this context? I only hear your valid-sounding criticisms. I don't hear any concrete, workable solutions or suggestions to improve the R and R. All of you apparently have only one motive, that of stopping the dam and inflicting damages to its financial viability. Your struggle here and elsewhere will ensure that the country is energy starved. You also oppose nuclear energy, thermal energy. How does the country make economic progress? Where do we go from here? You, however, draw a high level of international attention. You select a few ladies from land-owning families, dress them up in local dresses, take them abroad. There, they give fiery speeches against the Indian system, giving your version of exploitation going on in India. You get adequate applause and perhaps financial support. Your organisation will, in due course of time, also deteriorate and become another profession. How much will these villagers really gain from your confrontationist functioning? Shouldn't you too be subjected to a reality check?'

'General Sahib', reiterated Sanjay. 'Just invert your argument. What would happen to these villagers from such backward regions of Madhya Pradesh, if we were not agitating for them? Do they have any *Mai Baap*, except about a crore of Gods depicted in our mythological past? They, your employers, will suck their blood, make *ch…as* out of them. The entire government machinery lives on their bribes in this district and in Bhopal. The poor in India will have to forever bear the burden of democracy. Sir, this is the bottom line here.

'Don't we see the number of cars and SUVs of your private company attached with the relevant government officials, including MLAs and the police at the level of District Headquarters? Ostensibly, these vehicles are there to enable the officials to do the work for your project. Actually these vehicles are being used by family members of government authorities to go to religious shrines all around, including in the neighbouring States. All such expenses and much more are coming from the project costs. They are the stakeholder of this project and not the villagers.

'When the engineers blast the river bed and sides, some houses of the nearby villages crack, get damaged. The affected villagers ask for a few thousand rupees as compensation. They are shooed away. Come on sir, you know it all. Your company officials are misguiding the ignorant villagers and luring them to accept cash in lieu of agricultural land, which will get submerged. They should be giving them land for land. Your company does not have any land bank.

'These poor fellows, who have never seen a few lakh of rupees, are fully into a trap. The money will be spent by them and their land goes away for ever.'

'It is not so black and white as you put it', I fought back. 'Wherever site inspections prove that some houses have been damaged, compensations as per assessment, are paid. But when you instigate scores of people to demand compensation and agitate, when their houses are not damaged due to recent blasting, aren't you being unfair? You are teaching these people to demand false compensations. See, your main preoccupation is to oppose the project and damage its economic viability. As you do so, you get international recognition. While suspect Indian corporate ethics and motivations are part of the conflict between development project and the affected people, your role is also not as benign and idealistic as you make it look.'

'Okay', Nidhi interjected. 'Let us go deeper into this debate. Are these project-affected poor villagers stakeholders to this project for which their thousands-of-years-old villages are getting submerged, their agricultural lands submerged? No. This so-innocently called "'run of the river" project will submerge forty villages. This dam does not have any irrigation benefits. The electricity produced will not be lighting bulbs in any of the relocated villages. Its cost of production of electricity over a year's period will be too high for the villagers to afford. Big fish contractors from outside the district will harvest fish commercially from the vast water reservoirs created by the dam, after it devours all the forty villages, including agricultural land. Who knows now, how many more? So why should not the affected villagers oppose this dam? We are only empowering them and galvanising them to express their resentment. Dear General

Ssahib, this is war going on here. War of a different kind, than you have experienced. For third world countries, this is "The War" of the 21st Century. If this war is not waged, every development project in rural India will perpetuate abject poverty and encourage exploitation of these people. The entire plan on Rehabilitation and Resettlement is a bluff. These people will become even poorer than they are now. They have to fight this form of governance and profiteering.'

I watched in amazement, the contempt and hatred emanating from Nidhi as she added, 'Don't you understand the logic and relevance of Naxalism spreading all over the hinterland of rural India?'

'But then', I exclaimed, 'aren't these people a viable vote bank? How can any government ignore them as ruthlessly, as you are trying to explain?'

'Oh my God! There we go again to the dichotomy that is India', said an exasperated Sanjay. 'It is all so deviously simple. While doing a rudimentary, treacherous Rehabilitation and Resettlement, the powerful elements, the few landlords would be bought off, and the thousands of others will eventually be subdued. The actual vote bankers are the big landowners, they garner, build up the votes. It is all part of the brilliant strategies of those in power who have a vested interest in keeping people poor, uneducated or undereducated and dependent. Fifty per cent BPL cards are fake, half the rations of the rural public distribution system of over twenty million tons vanish into the black hole of black markets. Such is the black money which returns back to the rulers of the nation during elections.

'Politicians may win elections or lose them, every election makes them richer. This is the dance of democracy. Lord Shiva has not danced in such a destructive manner for at least a few millennium. Naxalism is the lap on which these angry, destitute people will eventually fall. Even there, they would be exploited for destabilising the country. We, the activists, are fighting a losing battle to prevent that. Don't you realise it General Sahib?

'Proposals to dish out subsidised food, free food, free electricity, waiving of lakhs of crores of loans, etc are all part of the comprehensive loot of the nation.'

While listening to the activists in a dusty, filthy, village in the interior of Madhya Pradesh, I recollected reading somewhere about Ambedkar. Ambedkar had denounced villages as cesspools of cruelty and prejudices. Dominant castes, who are the major land owners, continue acting like feudal lords even seventy years after freedom. Social barriers make it difficult for Dalits and Shudras to raise their heads.

No wonder, the best way to rule rural India is to buy off the rural landlords. But I reflected, this too is changing these days. But then at what pace and price? Where and what is India heading towards? Another old Hindi film song, I was fond of flashed in my mind:

Jinhe Naaz hai Hind par woh kahan hai,
Kahan hai, kahan hai, kahan hai?

(Where are those people who are proud of India,
Where are they? Where are they? Oh where are they?)

Lunch being served came as a good break for me. We all sat on a *duree*. The ladies of the joint family of the host laid down well-scrubbed steel *thali*es. Four small rounded *katori*s were neatly spread in a semi-circular fashion around each *thali*. One each was for the aromatic dal (lentils), curd, a mixed vegetable curry and a sweet dish. The ladies, with their heads covered, would pour the dishes into each *katori*. After this came hot *roti*es and rice.

As we were eating, Sanjay pressed on with the discussion. Now his tone was calmer. 'General Sahib, our meeting today in such a different environment has given us an opportunity, which we are happy about. At least, we see you and your Colonel roaming around in the heat, dust and rigours of the forty villages. We hardly see the real people who matter, from the industrialist and their officers who are the main figures of this project. They fear that in some villages, their vehicles will be stoned or they will be roughed up.'

I decided not to get provoked and kept quiet.

Nidhi concluded just as we were finishing the lunch. 'Sir, you will go back to your retired life soon. This job is not for you. Write a book, play golf, enjoy your well-deserved rest. All your life you must have been a proud Indian, ready to sacrifice all for its security. By the time you leave soon, you will experience a great disillusionment in your long-held pride for this country. External threat to national security would appear more identifiable and controllable than the looming threat to the internal security of India. The people who are posing the internal security threat to India are the most powerful heads of government, the rulers and their existing corrupt system. They are choking this nation.'

Finally, I had to get my say. I thanked the host and family members and concluded, 'The day I really feel that I am wrongly placed in this project, I shall quit. That is no issue at all. I noticed that you both, and the organisation you represent, have completely painted yourself white and others black. I cannot digest that. You used the word "they" so many times while telling me about all that is wrong in India. I am not sure whether this exclusive logic is correct. Your argument, though powerfully expressed, appears to be like a tennis game, somehow to put the ball in the other court.'

'Notwithstanding all that you have said, and the fact that I enjoyed this interaction with you both, I don't see any dilution in my deeply-held love and pride for my country. My country is too large, vast, multipronged, full of potential, capabilities, for individuals like you and me to condemn it. Incidentally, before we have the right to be ashamed of our country, we should start feeling ashamed of ourselves. We have made our country the way it is. I see no signs of introspection in you two. Your aim is to win debates. I am reminded of the Biblical sentence, To Thine Own Self Be True. As a military man, we never lose our spirits, our *josh* and resolve to serve the nation. No one can take that away from us. Defeats only raise our resolve and up the ante of our motivations. We are different. Some of your points though, were thought-provoking, I accept them. Namaste.'

I walked away, trying my best to give the two activists the impression that they could not influence me.

One day, a delegation of fishermen and boatmen, led by a tall, intelligent person wanted to meet me. This community formed a significant part of the total number of people belonging to the villages which were doomed to be submerged by the water reservoir the dam would create, once it becomes operational. The leaders of the delegation made very sensible and reasonable demands and a proposal that excited me. The local leader of this community was Mangat Ram. He was the Adhyaksh of the Machuara Sangathan. This community project would have converted a huge population of project-affected people into pro-dam lots.

The young leader addressed me confidently. 'Sirji', he said. 'We have been fishing the Narbada river for thousands of years. We have also been rowing our boats to take people across the river and earning a living. Now, this dam and the bridge constructed have affected our lives. But when the water reservoir is created due to the dam, it can also give us an advantage. The fish production in the water reservoir can be increased significantly.

'We have a legitimate right to be given fishing rights on the reservoir. If this is done, then a large number of project-affected people will become the beneficiaries and stakeholders in this dam. Public resentment and struggle against the dam will reduce significantly. We also propose that the project management and the Fishery Department of the State Government, together set up a fishery project next to the dam site, to be able to ensure that thousands of tons of additional fish can be produced and harvested. Through this project, we fishermen can form our own cooperatives, who would get the fishing rights. We also need a few modern fishing boats for deep-water fishing. Sir, please ensure that big fish contractors are not given fishing rights here. I have information that big fish contractors are already contacting the government. This will really create a very violent agitation in future, which can be avoided. Please help us. We are a peaceful community and do not want conflict. We only demand our right to fishing.'

I saw a great opportunity in this demand and proposal. A very viable Community Development Project could be planned and executed. A large chunk of the resentful, restless population would become stakeholders in the dam. I could really contribute towards this hydro-electric project and neutralise the anti-dam activists, who would have to accept the fact that people can be well resettled and benefit from the project. Twin issues of granting fishing rights and setting up of a fishery project will be real clinchers, game changers. Since the State government was so power deficit, it should be reasonable to expect that it would seize this opportunity, grant fishing rights, form the fishermen cooperatives. It had its own Fishery Department which could be directed to do this quickly. Opening of a fish breeding project and associated activities could have been easily implemented as part of the annual, rural development projects in the district.

The private company building the dam could shoulder part of the expense of this project, as well as provide a piece of land near the dam. It had acquired enough land around the periphery of the dam site. A perfect public-private cooperation and development. The dam itself was a public-private project.

I felt a fresh flow of adrenal, was full of *josh* and motivation. This was an opportunity with great potential and probability of success. I wrote out a paper on this project and sent it to concerned people. I spoke to the groups representing thousands of fishing community members. They too were excited. They promised full support for the dam if they become legitimate stakeholders of the project.

Surprisingly, response from all agencies was lukewarm. The senior officer of the Fishery Department, a lady bureaucrat, promised all help and guidance. She had adequate funds in her department for such projects. Some other fishery projects were already in execution elsewhere. When I asked the leader of the fishing community about my desire to see some of the other government fishery projects, he said that they were all on paper, badly implemented with no benefits. Going to see them will be a waste of time and a discouraging experience. I suggested that since this planned fishery project will be co-located adjacent to the dam, with part funding by corporate money, we all can monitor its implementation and ensure its success.

For six months, even after various letters, calls to the Fishery Department officials at all levels, there was no progress. Delegation of fishermen community from villages affected by the dam came back angry and frustrated. They suggested that the Project Management provide funds to bribe the officials, without which this project would not progress. Moreover, big fishing contractors were also active in ensuring that they got the contract. After all, they were big players who also possessed the infrastructure and wherewithal to harvest the vast quantity of fish that will accrue, to collect them and take them away in refrigerated vehicles. The private company building the dam could not afford to get involved in this system. Ultimately, only the government machinery could ensure the welfare of the people.

One afternoon, the senior Vice President of the private company undertaking the hydel project walked into my office room. He was a hard-working, harassed, technically brilliant guy, mostly stuck in his office. He was not a field-level manager and his leadership skills were limited. Though very well paid, his position was an unenviable one. In financial matters, at a personal level, he was very honest indeed. In professional sphere, he was too busy and occupied with balancing the larger interests of the project with the nonchalant, miserly attitudes of the business house which financed the project. I was convinced that he was fully aware of the writing on the wall regarding this project. The writing on the wall said clearly that the dam would surely be built, though belatedly. However, this dam will not produce any electricity for a long long time, due to non-implementation of the Rehabilitation and Resettlement package for the villages. This was one aspect on which the business house owning the dam was just not sincere enough. Neither were the government officials living in libertarian Disneyland, suffering from irrational dreams of an emerging India. Ground reality of rural India was being ignored arrogantly.

Asking for two cups of lemon tea to be sent in, I asked the much-harried gentleman about availability of some R and R funds to start a couple of my suggested resettlement projects. The senior Vice President replied in exasperation, '*Arrey*, we are starving of funds for the construction of the dam and you are inquiring about R and R funds. My blood pressure, cholesterol has gone up due to never-ending problems. I have no time for my family in Mumbai.'

I replied, 'Meanwhile, the villagers are getting angry at the lack of progress on R and R. The entire fishing community are getting frustrated. The anti-dam activists are getting more proactive.'

'Sahib, you must think of a strategy to defeat the plans of these activists. Please tap your military experience to devise some strategy. Do something to outsmart them', stressed the senior Vice President of the project.

'But Mr Chowdhary', I exclaimed, 'how can one devise a strategy from a position of weakness. You are aware that there are no funds to execute some plans which will increase employment and earning of the dam-affected villagers. When deprived, uprooted people lose hope, they lose the power of reasoning. They just listen and believe the anti-dam activists. I dare say that if I was in their situation, I would do the same. It is like a sick, frail, suffering man with low haemoglobin in his blood who looks helplessly at a white-robed, healthy-looking doctor, his saviour and pain reliever. Whatever the doctor says, becomes a source of revealed knowledge and hope. The anti-dam activists are telling them not to worry and to stay on in their villages, take whatever compensation which is offered. They will never have to leave their villages as this hydel project will not be allowed to succeed till the R and R is done to their entire satisfaction, duly monitored by the Supreme Court. They are also saying that powerful global entities are supporting their cause. Under these deteriorating circumstances, unless we do some substantive income-generation schemes, give the people some glimpses of our sincerity, we are losing this people's war against the project.'

'General Sahib', concluded Chowdhary, 'if the local agitation eventually does delay this hydel project indefinitely, why should any business concern spend money for R and R until the State government gives assurance that once the dam is constructed, they will ensure generation of electricity forthwith?' The dichotomy of India stared back at me, mocking at me and at all that I believed in my country.

The district-level government gradually started putting pressure, to prevent and resist some of the Community Development projects being formulated. This was done by subtle, indirect methods. Districts in Indian rural areas spend hundreds of crores every year for rural development and livelihood enhancement. Such massive amounts vanish in thin air because, how can one check ten paisa of delivery out of every rupee of hundreds and thousands of crores? Amidst this scenario, a private company executing visible, meaningful Community Development projects with a couple of crores on some villages could be very embarrassing to the government authorities.

I gracefully left the job. Nevertheless, it was a worthwhile experience, though a bit of an iconoclastic one. Despite all these experiences, at the evening of my life, I did not feel it right to disparage my country.

If one counts from the time India actually achieved economic independence in 1991, the nation was only over twenty years old. Problems were of massive proportions. People, after all, had the power to forestall and prevent major development projects which they perceived to be harmful to them. Major nuclear power projects, steel projects, manufacturing mega projects, even though urgently required for economic progress could be held up due to local resistance.

An anti-corruption non-violent movement, led by an old fragile social activist can shake up all the powerful government institutions, watched in amazement by the entire world. There have been several politicians, business honchos dragged to the jail, seen by the people on their TV screens in millions of Indian homes. Rural sophistication is visible to discerning observers at places when one sees young girls from poor families dressing up far better than hitherto, walking to school with confidence and grace. One sees India's scientific community, doctors, business and management experts doing the country proud. Indian students excelling in foreign universities is routine. The American President cautioning its youth to study harder, otherwise Indians and Chinese will take away the jobs from them, is another indicator. The loyal, disciplined, professionally-trained motivated Indian military, despite being not so well-equipped, always ready to take on any threat is a shining example. A pulsating, hyperactive media, brilliant higher judiciary as the watchdog of the Constitution of India—there are so many positives happening. Finally, despite many things to the contrary, political leadership at the apex level is very pragmatic in dealing with the deep complexities not only of governing India, but also with handling the international environment as well as a growing economy in an ever-globalising, flattening world space. I succumbed to the desirability of remaining positive amidst the encircling gloom. This was necessary to lead a healthy, retired life.

After all, I thought, I had lived an adventurous, purposeful life. I had tried to lead an upright life to the best of my ability, to try and make the least possible mistakes. I never considered myself to be an extraordinary, outstanding achiever. I was lucky to have done reasonably well. If one could be a good human being, a good son, a good husband, father, friend, a helping person, who tried hard to commit the least mistakes, one could claim to have had a life well lived.

I finally discovered the place where we would love to settle down. I built a nice comfortable house in a cantonment town in Madhya Pradesh, close to a premier training institutions of the Indian Army. I was among friends, among over one hundred retired military officers who were determined to enjoy and live quality lives together.

BIG AND SMALL

Footprints on the Eternal Sands of Time

In the world's broad field of battle, In the bivouac of Life, Be not like dumb, driven cattle! Be a hero in the strife!

—Henry Wadsworth Longfellow

Three years after my retirement, I decided to visit Gangotri. This was my second visit. I hiked around the mountains, a couple of hours walk from the Gangotri shrine. A few small isolated caves existed in the vicinity. One can always find a few sadhus living in such caves, self-contained, with food and meagre cooking facilities. They pray, meditate and spend some time alone, contemplating about life in the pristine, secluded region of quiet splendour and natural Himalayan symphony. I had visited these caves fifteen years earlier and chatted up a few such sadhus. I had realised that each person became a Sadhu for a different reason. A common factor which emerged, for many, was disappointments, failures in their personal lives. A deep pain caused many of them to seek spiritual explanations of the drudgeries of life. Somehow, I was not impressed by such futile escapism.

This time, however, I noticed a very serene, clean-shaven person, wearing a trouser, shirt and a warm pullover, sitting inside a cave.

He did not appear to be a typical sadhu. I was really impressed with the beautiful, radiant smile on the face of this person who was sitting, as if in meditation. He would close his eyes for a few minutes, then open them to admire the natural beauty outside, with his smile a constant. He appeared to be enjoying himself, rather than meditating.

I quietly waited outside the cave till I could draw the attention of this person. Soon he felt my presence. He folded his hands and asked me to sit next to him on a mat, which he unfolded. 'Welcome to my little abode my friend', he exclaimed with his mesmerising smile.

'Sorry, did I disturb you? My apologies to you', I said.

'Oh no', he laughed. 'In such a place like this, no meeting takes place by chance. I feel happy to meet you. I shall quickly brew some herbal tea for us. I am Partho Pal from West Bengal. I am a Buddhist.'

Partho lit a stove and put some water from a bucket nearby into a small kettle. Very intently, with great care he made tea, added some sugar. 'Sorry, there is no milk. But herbal tea doesn't need milk I suppose', he said, offering me a glass of tea.

As I sipped and relished a hot glass of tea, Partho watched me intently, smiling thoughtfully. 'Can we talk to each other informally? I am not a sadhu, so you need not be formal.'

I nodded in agreement. I noticed that Partho had the aura and demeanour which made me feel very comfortable. There was something in his persona which made him exceptional, which I could not fathom.

'For how long do you live in this cave?' I queried.

'I come here approximately once in two years, for the last ten years. I spend a few weeks, at times a month here. I love Gangotri and surrounding areas. May be there is some association with this place from one of my previous lives, who knows? There are so many rivers in all continents and parts of the world. They all originate from somewhere. Somehow, origins of rivers in India are so deeply associated with God. There is something mesmerising and deeply spiritual about the Gangotri region, the origin of the Ganges.'

'You are a deeply religious and spiritual person', I exclaimed.

'Oh no. I am an ordinary person. I have retired from government service. I worked in the Department of Agriculture in the State of

West Bengal. My father was a Head Master of a government school in Nadia District. After school hours, he used to provide free tuition to the children from poor families. Now a school is named after him in the village. My mother used to sing melodious bhajans in the local temple during festivals. We had a simple, happy life. The villagers living around us used to say that we are a family, blessed by God, because even my grandparents were very charitable, spiritual and deeply respected by all. We were not rich but were comfortable and well educated.'

'So, what is the connection?' between Nadia District of West Bengal and this cave near Gangotri, I asked.

'Oh, it is a simple connection. My grandparents had read a book written by a traveller about religious sites in the Himalayas. The book described in great detail mythological locations like Gangotri, Yamunotri, Kedarnath, Badrinath, Haridwar, Rishikesh etc. They wanted to visit Gangotri to see the origin of the Ganges. They could only come up to Haridwar and Rishikesh. My parents too yearned to come here. They could come up to Rudra Prayag, where the rivers Mandakini and Alakhnanda meet. Due to heavy landslides, they could not proceed ahead. Before my parents died, they had directed me to come to this place and offer Thanks Giving to God on their behalf.'

'I did come here after their death, ten years ago', continued Partho. 'I came, the first time only to fulfil the wishes of my parents and grandparents. Thereafter, I kept on coming here whenever I could. I also visited Tawang in Arunachal Pradesh and Bhutan. I became a Buddhist, not by conversion but by conviction. I do not consider Buddhism as a separate entity from Hinduism. I do not identify myself with the caste system in India somehow.'

'So, what do you realise or achieve by coming to this cave around Gangotri? I am curious to know this.'

'Friend, I feel connected to my parents and grandparents when I come and meditate here for a while. They were ordinary people, very noble souls who lived lives very honourably, helped others, lived by setting examples to others. They loved the country and its rich past. I also come here for Thanks Giving to God. God has given

me such noble, good parentage, who gave me excellent education and upbringing. I am happily married, with excellent, value-based children who are doing well and living their lives with honour and character. They pursue meaningful careers. What more can God give to anybody besides these blessings? There is something in the Himalayas which helps you connect with the Almighty. I feel rejuvenated here.'

I said pensively, 'I too got attracted to this place ever since I came here fifteen years ago. Somehow, I could not come here again, until now. I have retired from the Army after thirty-eight years in uniform. I suffered a complicated heart attack in 2005. I am a bit nervous and suffering from retirement blues, from the unpredictabilities of post-retirement life. I haven't planned my post-retirement life well.'

The radiant smile on Partho's face lit up my spirits. 'Tell me something about yourself, the life you lived so far. I want to listen to you. I am so glad we met here', said Partho patiently.

I described my childhood, my life in the Army with such natural enthusiasm as if I was speaking to a childhood friend. I was so mesmerised by Partho, I did not realise that a second glass of tea had already been consumed. Partho listened to me with rapt attention. He was a great listener. Just as I had finished speaking, Partho exclaimed, 'You lived your life rather well. You are a humble soul with an ingrained attitude for gratitude. We need to talk a lot. Please share a simple meal of *khichri* with me. I make it really well, though not as well as my late mother. Just watch me cook while we talk.'

Partho took out a bowl of raw rice and a small cup of dal. After mixing it up, he washed it and started boiling it on the stove. He added two spoons of ghee and threw some herbs into the boiling concoction.

'Interesting to hear your life story in brief my friend. You were not so worried during the 1971 war, as a young officer. You worked amidst stiff competition within the Army for thirty-eight years, since you passed out of the Indian Military Academy. You did well professionally, became a General. You faced extremely challenging situations, saw death and destruction from close quarters. You witnessed your brave soldiers and junior officers fighting bravely, dying or getting wounded in the process. You felt pain and anguish not only for those under your command, but also for innocent civilians caught in conflict situations. You are proud of your Regiment and the military traditions of Indian Army. After all this, you are now apprehensive of your post-retirement life. You are unable to reconcile with the heart attack you suffered, since you were always physically fit, never over indulged in life.'

Partho was now boiling two potatoes and peeling one onion.

'You know, since childhood, we nurture small small hopes, simple dreams, desires which grow embryonically as one lives on. Our dreams, desires, hopes get fulfilled and some of us start believing in God more and more. We pray, always asking for more. You kept on believing in God and kept your hopes and desires simple, realistic. As you grew in your highly competitive and adventurous, risky profession, the world became progressively complex.

'Take each decade of your life. The 1950s was a simple decade for a newly-created India savouring its independence. Your memories of childhood are emotively embedded in your mind. The 1960s was deceptively simple. India faced two conventional wars just as you were in the military institutions undergoing training. The 1970s was a decade of military glory for India, in which you were a young participant. The 1980s was a critical decade for your professional life wherein you had to build your career amidst stiff competition. The Sri Lanka operations came as a great, thankless challenge. The 1990s saw serious eruption of terrorism in Kashmir, as well as India going nuclear, which laid the foundation of grave future military challenges. The 2000s has been a decade of global upheaval, with South Asia becoming the most dangerous place in the world. Your military life changed seriously every decade of your service. As an infantry man, it affected you consistently. You literally lived with India while most others lived in India.'

'Yes, that is truly well summarised', said I smiling.

'I notice that you are not yet reconciled to your painful experience of a complex heart attack. In fact, you were so confident of your physical fitness, that you thought it was mere acidity. You never felt breathlessness. You delayed going to the hospital till the morning.

That increased the damage to your heart. You have not forgiven yourself for that mistake. Isn't it my friend?', queried Partho. 'You also blame God for not helping you out on this lapse.'

I nodded in agreement, marvelling at Partho's observation. This was so true, yet he did not realise it.

Partho looked deeply at me. 'It is time you forgive yourself. Reconcile, accept the fact that we all have to suffer our respective quota of pain and suffering. You were about fifty-seven years of age, when you got admitted in a hospital as an in-patient for the first time in your life. So you enjoyed excellent health till then. Isn't that itself a great positive in your happy, wholesome life? Many of your course-mates neither became a General nor enjoyed such a good health. Quite a few got killed or wounded in battle and encounters with the enemy. Some may have had unhappy married lives or their spouses died or their children suffered. So God has bestowed special favours on you.'

I replied, 'Yes, of course. I always realised this aspect of what you are saying with gratitude and humility. I, somehow, could not accept the heart attack with equanimity and grace.'

'Aah!' exclaimed Partho smiling. 'Your heart attack was a wake-up call to a new and better life, a qualitatively richer one after retirement, which was coming soon enough. Don't you see this? It was providentially timed, one year before retirement. You were a serving General and you had all the organisational support and attention. So many senior Generals in the hierarchy must have visited the Military Hospital, inquired about you. You also had one full year of service to recover significantly. You also enrolled to do a Doctorate in Management, which would have contributed towards your getting a suitable job immediately on retirement. You woke up to the fact that you must choose a suitable place to settle down, which you eventually did, constructed a beautiful house in the vicinity of a pristine, charming cantonment area.

'You wore the uniform at the age of twelve and after retirement, you settled down so close to an Army establishment, among over a hundred retired military officers. Don't you see the role of Divinity in all these developments? You didn't need to plan your retirement life. You never shaped your life since childhood. It was all shaped and choreographed by a higher power all along.

'You are a very lucky person. Enjoy life, relish your second innings after a significant first innings. You are, as you say, an excellent husband, a devoted father, a grateful son. You always tried to be loyal and protective of those under your command, you pray quite regularly. You, therefore, have lived your life quite well. What is your problem friend? You never claimed to be larger than life, you never tried seriously to be the best among your friends and colleagues. You probably pitched yourself, carefully-based on your honest analysis of your strengths and weaknesses. This humble approach took you to a fair level, may be a little more was expected or dreamt about. Am I right?'

'Yes, you are spot on', I confessed.

'Okay, we all are greater than the sum of our worldly achievements in life. We all need to maintain a Gratitude List. Some eminent lyricist coined this in Hindi which influenced me: *Kabhi Kisi Ko Mukammal Jahan Nahi Milta.* (Never does anybody get to live in a perfect world.)

'I am glad, we met in such a serene pure, natural surrounding. I do believe that this meeting is not just a chance meeting', exclaimed Partho. This time his radiant smile was blended with a touch of sadness.

'Partho, It was my fortune to have met you. You do not wear the robe of a typical saint. Today, I did meet a saint, a spiritual person. You may not realise how much you helped me today', I replied.

Needless to say, the simple *khichri* with a boiled potato was a very tasty meal indeed.

I exclaimed in admiration. 'Partho, I compliment you on your simple yet clear analysis of my life. You speak like a monk.'

'No, my friend', responded Partho. 'It is just that, sitting and being with myself in this serene, therapeutic environment, far removed from the din and bustle of life in the plains down below, enables me to think objectively. I love coming here for this reason.

'You know, billions of human beings live their lives on this planet, in their respective ways. On the sands of time, few outstanding, extraordinarily talented people, scientists, literary geniuses, economists, strategist and map makers etc leave huge footprints. Far more number of other remarkable people leave relatively smaller yet significant footprints on the sands of time, who are remembered in the history of their respective countries, regions. A very large number of good human beings, who lived their lives well, rendered service to society, brought up good children, created good families, were kind to fellow human beings, spread happiness, also left very small footprints on the sands of time. But their numbers are larger than the sum of the first two types of footprint makers. Their collective impact on the sands of time are no less significant. If you, me and others could become part of these smaller footprints, we have lived our lives very well. A far greater number of humanity spend their lives living only for themselves, at any cost to the rest of the world and environment, and leave no footprints on the sands of time. They despoil humanity. Many of these people are at the helm of power and authority. This has been the eternal truth of humanity.

'So, you see, whether it is to be Satyug or Kalyug, depends on this eternal truth. Human beings, and not any divine power, are the empowered, chief choreographers of Satyug or Kalyug. This is what I learn from my own thoughts, amidst the pristine environment of the Himalayas. Therefore, if you, me and others have lived our lives in a good manner and have been contributors towards the betterment of humanity, then we have lived our lives well', smiled Partho.

'But Partho, what about the large chunk of humanity who are too poor, frail, disempowered, diseased, living in utter despair, dying in millions daily', I asked.

'Friend, I have no prescription for this cruel reality. No scripture has been convincing enough on this matter to any rational human being. Coming to the present times, I feel that almost seventy years of sub-performance in governance—our character deficit so far, our shallow depth of patriotism and leadership deficit—are responsible. The pain and anguish of the suffering masses have not been expressed enough and thus taken for granted. People in India are doing what they have historically been doing. Waiting for leaders of merit, grit and determination, who love this nation deeply.

'Just as demand leads naturally to supply, the people have to firmly express their desire for a better system, better leadership, good governance. The voice and anger of the people will enable such leaders to emerge. They are somewhere in India's horizon. When they emerge, India will start changing. It will happen.'

'The time for change is coming soon. How it will play out, I wonder. Our deep-rooted democracy may ensure that it will happen relatively peacefully. Meanwhile, India's immediate neighbourhood needs to be carefully watched. Changes usually do not happen peacefully.

'In fact, whenever there is a revolution in the hearts and minds of people, new ways of thinking takes root. Politicians in a democracy are always afraid of the tsunami in hearts and minds of voters. Threat of becoming a nobody is the only thing that rattles them.'

I concluded, 'Partho, finally one can gauge how well one has lived one's life by asking the following questions:

How well have I tried to live my life?

How well I have loved in life?

How much did I matter to others while I lived my life?

'I feel that experience is mostly about a collection of mistakes and about learning from them. I, as a military man, feel that patriotism in its pristine form is old-fashioned and Old is Gold. It is about *Naam* which means honour, *Namak* which is loyalty and *Nishan* which means cause, identity. Any country which nurtures the concept of *Naam, Namak* and *Nishan* will become a great nation. This is my belief, as per which, we have a long way to go.'

Partho gave a smile. 'Walk into the sunset, smiling my friend. We all have to', he said. His smile was like a curve which straightens out one's worries and confusions.

A decade after my retirement, India's political scenario became positively different. The years 2013-14 would be remembered in the future history of India as a revolutionary one. With only a very few exceptions, revolutions have been accompanied by extreme violence. India's independence struggle and South Africa's struggle against apartheid have been the exceptions so far. The scientist, Albert Einstein, said, 'The world, as we have created it, is a process for our thinking. It cannot be changed without changing our thinking.'

From the 1950s there has been revolutions in the hearts and minds of the people in various parts of the country. These started in different time frames, different decades. These were not collective in nature.

What is the significance of 2013-14? For the first time, a revolution in the hearts and minds of the entire people of India has taken form in unison. This is an unique revolution of its own kind in the world. It is a revolution within a democratic framework. People are too indignant, impatient to change India, unshackle it from the deadly grip of misgovernance, loot and extreme poverty. Without this revolution, demographic dividend will turn into violent, uncontrollable revolution.

Such an unique revolution needs an unique leader. A modern 21st Century, customised leader. But such a leader needs a group of matching leaders, both at the national and State levels. Where are they? Surely they will emerge. India has never lacked such people. They have to be google searched and empowered. Will that happen? Will the high aspirations, which have embryonically grown in the hearts and minds of people of India, be met to a significant extent? I hope so. God save India from being forever in the third world, if this revolution does not succeed.

In this real-life story, some people have lived with India over the last six decades. Most of the billion plus Indians have got used to the melancholy of living in India, accepting the harsh status quo. Now the revolution in the hearts and minds of increasing numbers of Indians have made them determined to live with India by shaping its destiny as stakeholders. They only need able leadership.

My story, as lived through, also reveals a larger theme. The people of South Asia's eight countries are now demanding less politics, better governance and faster development. They are increasingly asking for stakeholdership in speedy development. The people of India must lead to create this popular tsunami. SAARC must become a region where people drive their leaders and bureaucrats to change the status quo. A popular movement is building up. Imagine what a massive transformation may arise from a hopeless horizon. We are seeing a revolution of the hearts and minds collectively brewing, covering a region which has one fourth of the world population and nearly half of the world's poor. The only need is to apply one's ability to guide this movement, manage it wisely to steer it to its logical conclusion.

If any country of this region gets left out of this enterprise, then the fault will not lie in their stars. Such a country either boards the train or misses it. Just as North Korea may have to be left behind in the future rise of Asia, during this century.

Under the current leadership, India needs to display its new-found culture of strategic thinking. One critical aspect of strategic thinking relates to the use of military power to achieve critical national objectives, as well as earning international applause while doing so.

In the past, India did so in Maldives during 1988. A tiny, but strategic nation-state of Maldives was threatened with a coup by mercenaries. India's military intervention to prevent this was globally recognised as a model for benign security role in the Indian Ocean. It was a defining moment for India. The coup was organised by a Sri Lankan insurgent group. They infiltrated into the capital of Male and took control of key areas of the city. They failed to capture President Abdul Gayoom.

The strategic angle of the crises for India lay in the fact that Maldives requested for military assistance from India, USA, Britain, Pakistan, Sri Lanka, Malaysia and other Asian states. For a change, New Delhi responded with uncharacteristic speed and decisiveness, clearly indicating to the world that it was India's prerogative and responsibility. India intervened in its own national interest, clearly telling the world that this part of the Indian Ocean was critical to India's security interests. As many as 300 Indian special forces were flown from Agra and paradropped with great precision on an island near Male. Additional forces followed. It was a short, swift, professional intervention. As soon as the insurgents were captured or overcome, they were handed over for trials to the Maldives Forces. The Indian Army withdrew immediately after that.

Later, there have been the examples of viable evacuation of citizens from Lebanon and Libya. The present Prime Minister displayed his strategic insight about use of Indian military capabilities on two major global crises situations, within one year of his Prime Ministership. What makes his case more worthy is the fact that this was his first exposure beyond Gujarat to politics at the national and international level. That shows the potential.

India's massive security operations in war-torn Yemen have earned it global appreciation—with twenty-three countries seeking India's help in evacuating their nationals amidst grave risks is testimony to this. Here was no room for delay, procrastination, no *babugiri,* not much of file noting. Delay could have been fatal. Split-second decisions had to be taken. A retired Army Chief was right there on the spot. Indians and foreigners were pulled out amidst gun fire and bombs. Massive use of the Indian Air Force, the Indian Navy, extensive diplomatic consultations with Saudi Arabia and the USA, made the rest of the world watch the entire operation with deep appreciation. No red tape, no bureaucracy, no dithering. This heralded a new, emerging India under a dynamic leader. The hearts and minds of people were awakened, self-pride, national dignity were restored. Indians realised their own potential capabilities to an extent not realised so comprehensively earlier.

The latest strategic initiative in a global scale was launched recently, during the enormous earthquake in Nepal in 2015. Two dozen massive military aircraft and helicopters, along with National Disaster Relief Force teams and Indian Army detachments were used for rescue operations on a war footing. All channels of the Indian media sent their teams swarming all over Nepal, constantly reporting about the situation. The great strategic utility of the recently acquired C-17 Globemaster-III and C-130 Super Hercules heavy aircrafts were displayed to the world. This was a new India, ready to respond to any crisis in the strategic neighbourhood in a quick span of time. Army medical teams, surgical teams spanned out into the interiors of Nepal. MEA officials, North and South Block bureaucrats, realising the new heights of national aspiration, raised their levels of performance adequately. The Indian aviation industry rose to the challenge.

India's neighbourhood realised that when 1.25 billion Indians are determined to help them during such crisis, they have benign leadership in South Asia. India's present Army Chief, who is himself from India's Gurkha Regiment, was in constant touch with his Nepalese counterpart to provide assistance. This is what grand strategy is all about.

If similar joint statesmanship is displayed on the political, economical and other spheres of activities, then South Asia can rise like a phoenix from the cesspool that it is in, at the moment. Then, and only then, will the hearts and minds of the people in this subcontinent be healed. Conflict, differences over respective aspects of national interests will not vanish, but will became relatively more manageable. Competing interests will get intensified. India need neither fear competition nor confrontation.

Is India already a strategic player with commensurate capabilities and intentions?

Not yet. It appears though that it is well on its way to becoming one. Its strength to sustain its efforts to become one will be severely tested in the near future. The real and difficult journey for Nepal's recovery in medium and long term has commenced after the dust and tragedy has been absorbed. Soon, international donors will fade away to deal with other calamities in some other regions.

The strategic pace for South Asia will became a serious competition between India, China and to a lesser extent Pakistan. As far as Nepal is concerned, the entire nation is being rebuilt and multiple donors and helpers will be required by them. Can India and China display astute joint leadership now, when China's ability to help Nepal is too vast. While India talks too much about its assistance, China quietly works and without fanfare, tries to touch the hearts and minds of the Nepalese people. That is a crucial difference. In strategic space, no lunches are free, except the initial ones during a calamity.

This brings into focus the relationship between 'intentions' and 'capabilities' of nations during strategic power plays. If there are ambitions, intentions, but not commensurate capabilities, then one can at best be a runner-up. Is India trying to force the pace of becoming a strategic player before it has built up its commensurate capabilities? Seven decades of bad governance is now showing us the mirror.

Again, as in all past decades, there are too many questions and two few answers. Attempt to answer some questions itself raises many more questions. It is a case of Past Imperfect, Present Positive and if cards are played well, Future Bright. The new Prime Minister can make it happen. India has to help him to achieve that. Do the people of India have it in them, to raise their levels? The jury is out and unclear on this. Just expecting one man to raise India to such strategic and economic heights is a foolish dream. We need to think deep.

It is not to say and belittle ourselves that there were no green shoots during the first seven decades after independence. There were many indeed. But we need to compare in a fair manner. In the Fifties, we had an eminent Nehru, a great Patel etc. Malaysia (Malaya) had Tungku Abdur Rahman, Singapore had Lee Kuan, Indonesia had Sukarno.

Seven decades later, if one visits all these countries, observes their infrastructure, governance, discipline, rule of law and order, traffic discipline, penchant for patently standing in a queue, awaiting one's turn, civic sense, an Indian should feel unsatisfied and introspect. Only those who are arrogant and shameless would not feel a tinge of shame.

Now, in the second decade of the 21st Century, India is steadily, though slowly, undergoing a perceptional upgrade. Green shoots of hope are denting the prevailing negativism, which I have been pontificating about. While China has successfully made the leap into the prosperous zone, India is trying to demolish the old stereotypes. The process still is very slow. A slow but sure revolution largely within its democratic framework suits India. That is what can be managed and sustained.

It was said that when China awakens, the world will tremble. May be it is equally true that when India awakens, humanity will be better, safer, fairer. The people of India must put their politicians under sustained aspirational pressure for change. Revolution must come from the hearts and minds of the people at large. That is the best way to demolish third-rate stereotypical political leadership and send it into oblivion. This low bar must be raised so high that lesser mortals will find it impossible to enter politics. Therefore, the 1950 Bollywood song, *Jinhe Naaz Hai Hind Par Who Khan Hai,* will finally find an apt answer.

What is it that a country like India lacks today?

Such an analysis is too vast a subject. But essentially, lack of gross national character, discipline and propriety and at the deepest layer, lack of genuine patriotism at the higher level of society, seems obvious.

The hierarchy of values appears to be a very small ladder with too few steps. In that also, national pride seems to have a very small space. This was aptly displayed during the 2010 Commonwealth Games, to only quote one example. If these deficiencies did not exist, then India could have been more sensitive towards existence of such abject poverty. Our belief in the wrong interpretation of the caste system perhaps convinced our hearts and minds that it is the proclaimed destiny of the lower caste to remain so poor and miserable. That is why, most poverty alleviation proposals provide lucrative new opportunities to those in power for corruption.

One must concede that there are some well-dones in a callous system of rapacious governance. Many success stories are visible amongst scientists, business ventures, innovations, start ups, an efficient military institution, Election Commission, in flashes amidst the judiciary, honest bureaucrats who carry on despite being subjugated, harassed, killed. There are more such successes today than ever before.

The purpose of parliamentary democracy is to prevent social unrest. Mere voting rights sans development and a credible, fair redistribution system, is no longer a long-term safety valve. Seventy years of sub-governance has brought India into a new threshold.

That threshold is the ignition in the hearts and minds of Indians. As of now, their determination for change is formidable. As yet, they largely hope for a non-violent change.

China is not a democracy. But if its governance, economic might, political centralisation, combined with economic liberalisation, enables it to reduce poverty more than India can, then the Chinese people will bear with their lack of political democracy and allow the process of economic growth to continue. As the Chinese people become economically better, empowerment will automatically happen. While the Chinese political leaders understand their ground realities, one also wonders how serious are the Indian political leaders on such issues?

If in any society, inequality not only persists but grows wider, violence is an embedded reality. More violence leads to more inequality.

Violence cannot also be countered by classical non-violence either. Judicious management of a violent response should be a part of a much larger response, based on internal roots and causes. The solution cannot be simplistic. Addressing the aggrieved hearts and minds of masses could be the most complex challenge of the civilised world. The darkness is internal, and solution does not lie outside in the courtyard.

When a democratic state betrays its people and the Constitution, the people will want to betray the system and ensure its collapse. The problem is, that the people will have no idea or control over what will happen thereafter.

People have the power to generate chaos. Ultimately, good governance is the only way. Democracy, as it is practiced in India, will not provide good governance. If China manages to handle the revolution in the hearts and minds of the Chinese better than India, then democracy will collapse in India. And that is the last thing which should happen. With the Chinese per capita income of 6,800 dollars, compared to India's 1,500 dollars, India is simmering at its foundation. Can democracy lose out to autocracy in this Asian century? China appears determined to prove this point.

If so, then the 21st Century is China's century. The runners-up nations will be very distinctively distant, to make the race rather uncompetitive. Presently, the only hope to catch up with China and beat it rests in the probability of an implosion within China. This is a defeatist approach. China's national ambition is to be the most powerful nation in the globe. Doubt this at your own peril. India's futuristic vision is limited to its democratic election process of every five years.

India's national interest is always consigned to five years of rigorous imprisonment. India is a status quo nation. People want to break this status quo. Wither wisdom, sobriety, grand vision and patriotic resolve? If all these facts do not make my readers a little nervous, then the author salutes your superiority. Hope Asia does not say, 'Good Bye India. You could have been a great power.'

If a person, who wants to join the Indian military as an officer, during an interview of a selection board says that he wants to join the Army, Navy or Airforce to serve the nation, he is rejected. Politicians keep insisting that they join politics to serve the nation. The starting point needs to be corrected. If democracy and good governance does not marry and settle down till death makes them part, there can be no democracy in real terms. Presently, in India, they are divorced, not even in a live-in relationship, caught in the line of people's ire.

The Indian military institution has also developed, over the past decades, a deep-rooted persecution complex for very genuine reasons. It is not only the civilian community which has suffered inadequate governance over the last seven decades. The military community too has suffered from a short-sighted leadership. In fact, being bound by stringent rules and the compulsions of discipline, they have suffered more. It now looks up to the present Prime Minister for redressal.

The correction needs a high-quality row of leadership. The trouble is that people in India are conveniently outsourcing this responsibility entirely on the shoulder of its present Prime Minister. An one-man army to sort out the problems of 1.25 billion Indians. A mythological Abhimanyu, who will alone enter the *chakravyuh*. Abhimanyu died in the process. No, he was assassinated. He dared to enter but knew not how to come out. His entire army waited outside the *chakravyuh*. It was the most non-strategic part of the battle.

Things don't work that way. You cannot even convince Indians to wear helmets on two wheelers, observe basic rules and laws, be less corrupt. The governance, at large, is seriously in business of business. Democracy is all about elections, rights, not responsibilities. Character lies only in its mythological scripts. Hundreds of millions of Indians defecate everywhere, anywhere in the open, at times in the most visible places. The present Prime Minister has to resolve all this, resting on his lonesome shoulders. Even offering constructive criticism is treated by his *bhakts* as anti-national. The Prime Minister needs support of the nation. The last thing he needs is blind adulation. He is no Moses who will lead 1.25 billion people out of the cesspool. He is a leader who needs many more layers of good leaders as well as a constructive opposition. He needs the hearts and minds of the people to assist him in doing his best and bring about a major change in a rotting system. As long as he is trying, India has hope. The situation is, however, tenuous, slender. India has to go through this *Agni Pariksha*. At present, the hope is that it will.

The hearts and minds of the people in India seem to be cautioning those who govern India, in what WB Keats said, 'Tread softly, because you tread on my dreams.' This may be the last battle for power of the remnants of a defunct breed of those whose job was to govern India well.

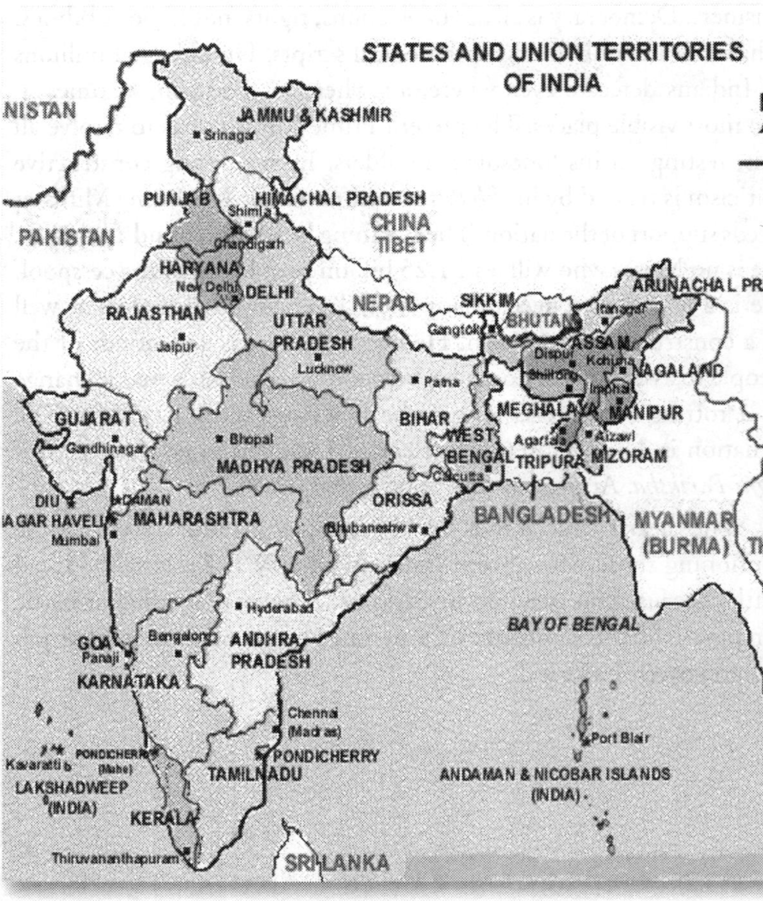
STATES AND UNION TERRITORIES
OF INDIA
NISTAN
JAMMU & KASHMIR
Srinagar
PUNJAB
HIMACHAL PRADESH
Shimla
PAKISTAN
Chandigarh
CHINA
TIBET
HARYANA
New Delhi
DELHI
NEPAL
SIKKIM
ARUNACHAL PRA
RAJASTHAN
Jaipur
UTTAR
PRADESH
Lucknow
Gangtok
BHUTAN
Itanagar
ASSAM
Dispur
Kohima
Shillong
NAGALAND
Imphal
Patna
MEGHALAYA
MANIPUR
GUJARAT
Gandhinagar
Bhopal
BIHAR
WEST
BENGAL
Agartala
Aizawl
MIZORAM
TRIPURA
MADHYA PRADESH
Calcutta
DIU
DAMAN
ORISSA
BANGLADESH
MAHARASHTRA
MYANMAR
(BURMA)
Mumbai
Bhubaneshwar
Hyderabad
BAY OF BENGAL
GOA
Panaji
Bangalore
ANDHRA
PRADESH
KARNATAKA
Chennai
(Madras)
Port Blair
PONDICHERRY
Kavaratti
TAMILNADU
ANDAMAN & NICOBAR ISLANDS
(INDIA)
LAKSHADWEEP
(INDIA)
KERALA
Thiruvananthapuram
SRI LANKA

enter but knew not how to come out. His entire army waited outside the *chakravyuh*. It was the most non-strategic part of the battle.

Things don't work that way. You cannot even convince Indians to wear helmets on two wheelers, observe basic rules and laws, be less corrupt. The governance, at large, is seriously in business of business. Democracy is all about elections, rights, not responsibilities. Character lies only in its mythological scripts. Hundreds of millions of Indians defecate everywhere, anywhere in the open, at times in the most visible places. The present Prime Minister has to resolve all this, resting on his lonesome shoulders. Even offering constructive criticism is treated by his *bhakts* as anti-national. The Prime Minister needs support of the nation. The last thing he needs is blind adulation. He is no Moses who will lead 1.25 billion people out of the cesspool. He is a leader who needs many more layers of good leaders as well as a constructive opposition. He needs the hearts and minds of the people to assist him in doing his best and bring about a major change in a rotting system. As long as he is trying, India has hope. The situation is, however, tenuous, slender. India has to go through this *Agni Pariksha*. At present, the hope is that it will.

The hearts and minds of the people in India seem to be cautioning those who govern India, in what WB Keats said, 'Tread softly, because you tread on my dreams.' This may be the last battle for power of the remnants of a defunct breed of those whose job was to govern India well.

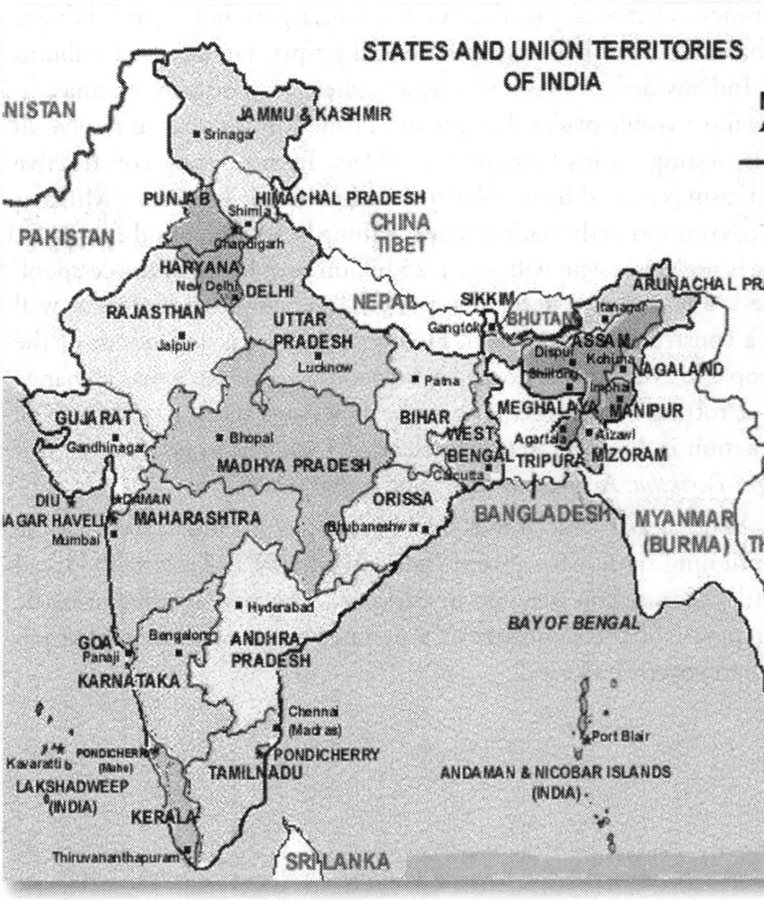
STATES AND UNION TERRITORIES OF INDIA
NISTAN
JAMMU & KASHMIR
Srinagar
PUNJAB
HIMACHAL PRADESH
Shimla
CHINA
TIBET
PAKISTAN
Chandigarh
HARYANA
New Delhi
DELHI
NEPAL
SIKKIM
ARUNACHAL PRA
Itanagar
RAJASTHAN
UTTAR PRADESH
Gangtok
BHUTAN
ASSAM
Jaipur
Lucknow
Dispur
Kohima
NAGALAND
Shillong
Imphal
Patna
MEGHALAYA
MANIPUR
GUJARAT
BIHAR
WEST BENGAL
Agartala
Aizawl
Gandhinagar
Bhopal
TRIPURA
MIZORAM
MADHYA PRADESH
Calcutta
DIU
DAMAN
ORISSA
BANGLADESH
MYANMAR (BURMA)
AGAR HAVELI
MAHARASHTRA
Mumbai
Bhubaneshwar
Hyderabad
BAY OF BENGAL
GOA
Panaji
Bangalore
ANDHRA PRADESH
KARNATAKA
Chennai (Madras)
Port Blair
PONDICHERRY
Kavaratti
PONDICHERRY (Mahe)
TAMILNADU
ANDAMAN & NICOBAR ISLANDS (INDIA)
LAKSHADWEEP (INDIA)
KERALA
Thiruvananthapuram
SRI LANKA

Theatres of Conflict

Theatre of Conflict

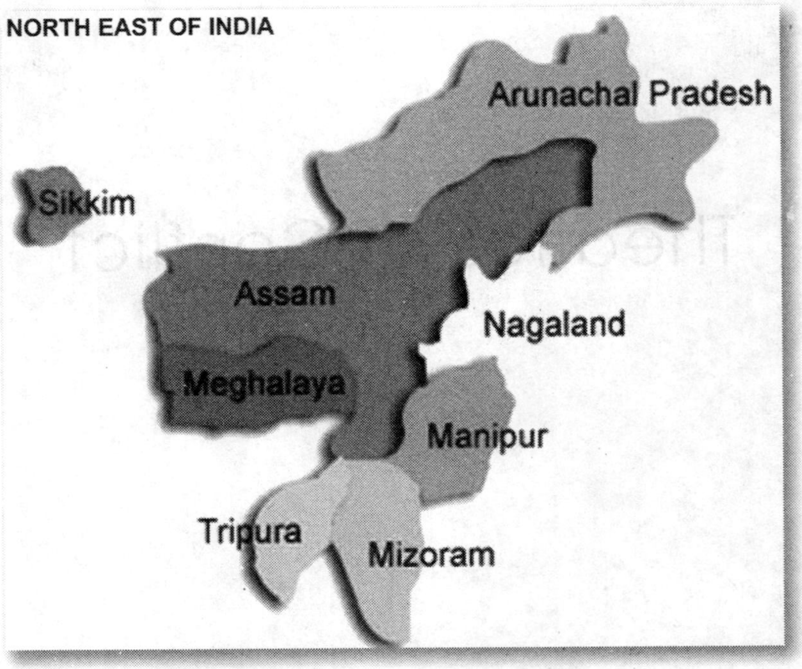

Theatre of Conflict

Theatre of Conflict

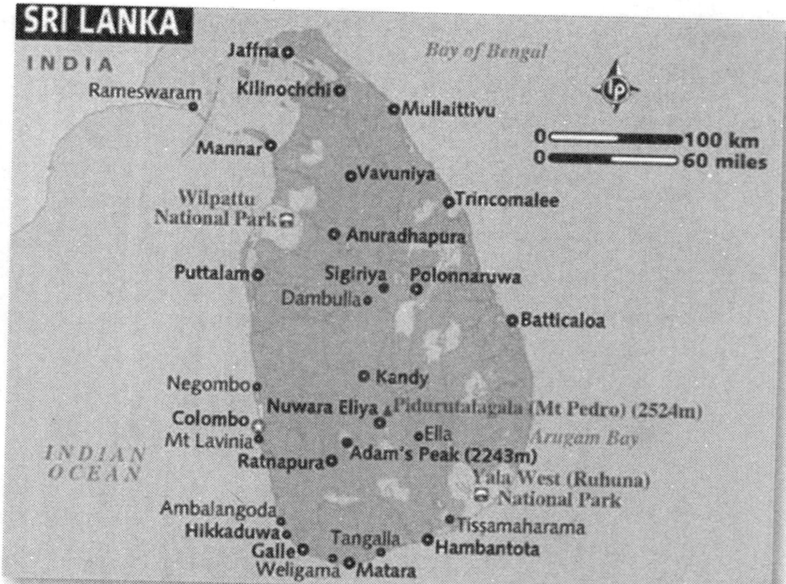

Theatre of Conflict

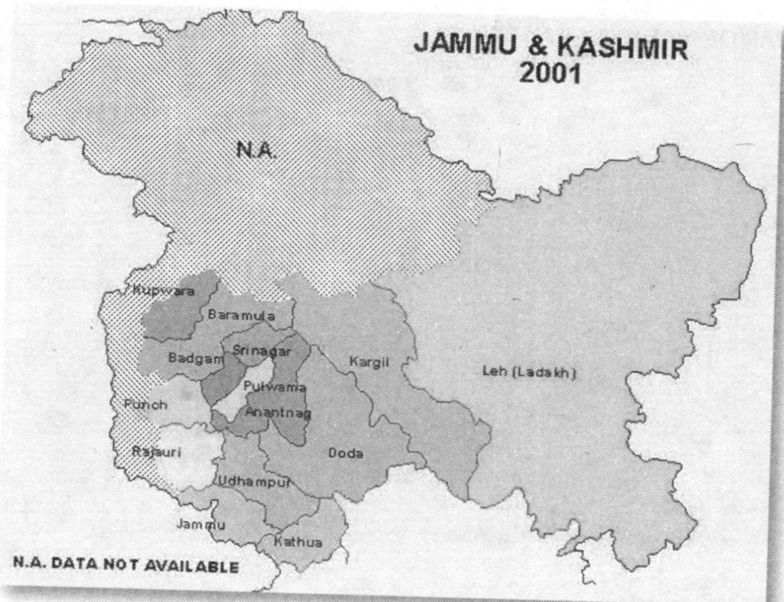

Theatre of Conflict

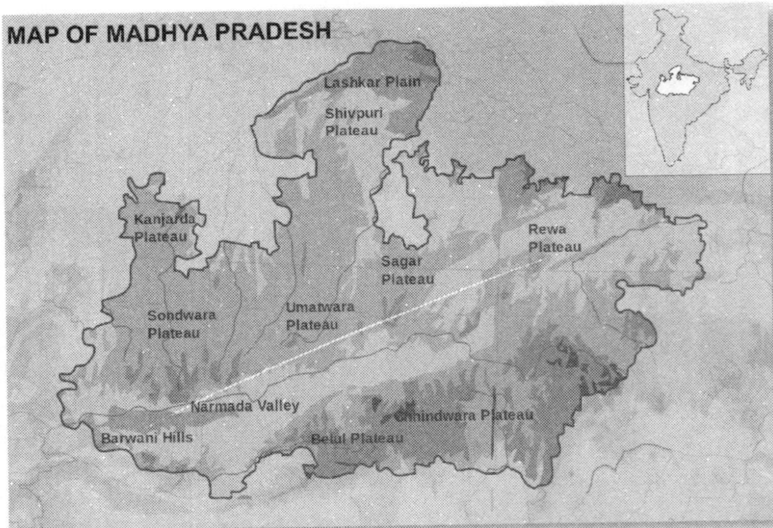